People to Know

Yo-Yo Ma

A Cello Superstar Brings Music To the World

Lisa A. Chippendale

Enslow Publishers, Inc.

40 Industrial Road	PO Box 38
Box 398	Aldershot
Berkeley Heights, NJ 07922	Hants GU12 6BP
USA	UK

http://www.enslow.com

Library of Congress Cataloging-in-Publication Data

Chippendale, Lisa A.
Yo-Yo Ma : a cello superstar brings music to the world / Lisa A. Chippendale.—
1st ed.
p. cm. — (People to know)
Summary: Tracks the life and career of violoncellist Yo-Yo Ma, a child
prodigy who grew to become world famous for his playing ability, as well
as for experimenting with different kinds of music and performance.
Includes bibliographical references (p.) and index.
ISBN 0-7660-2286-2
1. Ma, Yo-Yo, 1955– .—Juvenile literature. 2. Violoncellists—Biography—
Juvenile literature. [1. Ma, Yo-Yo, 1955- . 2. Violoncellists. 3. Chinese Americans—
Biography.] I. Title. II. Series.
ML3930.M11C45 2004
787.4'092—dc22

2003014972

Printed in the United States of America

10 9 8 7 6 5 4 3 2

To Our Readers
We have done our best to make sure all Internet Addresses in this book were active and
appropriate when we went to press. However, the author and the publisher have no control over and assume no liability for the material available on those Internet sites or on
other Web sites they may link to. Any comments or suggestions can be sent by e-mail
to comments@enslow.com or to the address on the back cover.

Every effort has been made to locate all copyright holders of material used in this book.
If any errors or omissions have occurred, corrections will be made in future editions of
this book.

Illustration Credits: © Corel Corporation, p. 13; AP/Wide World, pp. 4, 9,
18, 27, 36, 42, 55, 58, 60, 63, 67, 76, 77, 83, 86, 93; Don Perdue, p. 50;
Oumasan morin khuur instrument and photo by Okamoto, Koji (Poroniu,
Kyoto), Original drawing of horse head by Saga, Haruhiko (Throat-Singing
Society, Sapporo), p. 85; Photo by Kathy Kmonicek, p. 69; Photofest, p. 47;
Warner Bros. TV, p. 88; Photo by Woodrow Leung, p. 24.

Cover Illustration: William Coupon

Contents

Yo-Yo Ma

Inspired by Bach

A man strides through the crowd in Times Square, New York City. He is dressed in a black shirt, dark pants, and sunglasses. He carries a large brown instrument case and a folding chair. Crossing the street, he stops in the middle of an intersection on a wide traffic island. Cars whiz by on both sides. Skyscrapers and neon billboards tower in the background. The man sets up the chair, then puts his instrument case on a low wall. Opening it, he removes a highly polished cello. In its place he puts a handwritten Thank You sign to let passersby know that he is hoping for donations. He then sits down in the chair and begins to play. The music is familiar to most classical music fans and unknown to everyone else: It is the Sixth Suite for Unaccompanied Cello by Johann Sebastian Bach (1685–1750).

Millions of Americans saw this scene in April 1998—but not in Times Square. They saw it on their local PBS station as part of *Six Gestures*, a short film in the six-film series called *Inspired by Bach*. The cellist was none other than Yo-Yo Ma, considered by many to be the greatest cellist in the world today.

Why was Ma scrounging for change in Times Square as part of a film rather than appearing on stage with a world-class orchestra? Because unlike the majority of classical musicians, who spend their careers seeking perfection in concert halls, Yo-Yo Ma is always interested in taking risks and exploring different kinds of music and ways of performing.

The six suites written by Bach for solo cello are very important to Yo-Yo Ma. Each suite is made up of six different sections, called movements, and is about twenty to thirty minutes long. The suites were among the first pieces of music that Ma learned when he started playing the cello at age four. He recorded all six suites soon after he became a professional cellist, and the recording won him his first Grammy Award. One of the movements from the Fifth Cello Suite was the last piece of music Ma played for his father before he died.

In the early 1990s, Ma decided he wanted to see how creative artists who were not musicians would interpret the cello suites.[1] He approached film directors, dancers, and a garden designer, among others, about making a series of films based on the six cello suites by Bach. They agreed, and the *Inspired by Bach* project was the result. In *Six Gestures*, the film about the Sixth Cello Suite, Ma chose to work with well-known British ice dancers Jayne Torvill and Christopher Dean. The pair dominated world ice-dancing competition in the early 1980s. Torvill and Dean invented new routines for each movement of the Sixth Suite.

Six Gestures is like a documentary and a music video rolled into one. After beginning with Ma playing Bach in Times Square, the film changes settings and even characters. The next scene features an actor playing Bach as a young man. The character talks about his life as a musician and his family. The actor appears throughout the film, giving insight into Bach's life and how it affected the music he wrote.

The highlights of the film are Torvill and Dean. They glide across the ice during slow, soft movements and execute precise turns and fancy footwork during the dance-inspired movements of the Sixth Suite. For most of the film, they skate on ice surrounded by pillars and curtains, but sometimes director Patricia Rozema uses computer images to show them leaping across the face of a building or twirling through the sky. The director also plays with the lighting to create different moods, sometimes putting the two skaters in near darkness or blurring the focus to create a soft image.

Yo-Yo Ma himself is also on camera throughout the film. Sometimes he speaks about Bach, but most of the time he is playing his cello. The camera often shows his long fingers rushing up and down the fingerboard (neck) of the cello, or his bow moving deftly across and between the strings. Although he starts out in Times Square, he does not stay there for the entire film. Sometimes he is shown in black and white playing in a church, and other times he plays in full color on the gravel-coated roof of a city building with skyscrapers as his backdrop.

Even though the scenes change often throughout the film, director Rozema reminds the viewer that it began in a city. Words that look like graffiti on city walls provide information about Bach or comments on the music. Once information even appears printed on the side of a truck. Truck drivers stop and talk to the camera about Bach.

The film ends where it began: in Times Square. Ma finishes playing, pockets the coins tossed into his cello case, packs up, and makes his way back through the crowd.

Ma made the films for television so that he could bring Bach to a new audience, one that avoids concert halls featuring traditional classical music.[2] He also created the *Inspired by Bach* project to help him find new inspiration for the cello suites while collaborating with artists from nonmusical fields.

Not all music and film critics liked *Six Gestures*. Some criticized Rozema's decision to include the character of Bach in the film. One reviewer even said that cutting to the actor "mucked up" the attractive scenes featuring Torvill and Dean.[3] Others thought that Ma looked staged and unrealistic playing in Times Square.

Ma did not care what critics thought about the film and the *Inspired by Bach* project. "It made me an

Ma asked Jayne Torvill and Christopher Dean, shown here in the 1994 Olympics, to interpret Bach's Sixth Suite in dance.

infinitely richer person, and I think a better musician," he said. "No matter what people said about the project—and it raised a lot of eyebrows—I'll never regret having done it."[4]

Although Yo-Yo Ma was trained from an early age to be a classical cello player, the *Inspired by Bach* film series was just one of his many adventures outside the boundaries of the traditional concert hall.

Choosing a "Big Instrument"

Yo-Yo Ma's childhood was full of music. Both of his parents were musicians. His father, Hiao-Tsiun Ma, was a violinist, composer, and music teacher. His mother, Ya-Wen Lo, was a singer. Hiao-Tsiun Ma was from a town near Shanghai, China, about halfway down China's coastline. Ya-Wen Lo was from Hong Kong, an island off the coast of China. Until 1997, Hong Kong was controlled by the British government.

Hiao-Tsiun and Ya-Wen met in the early 1940s at Nanjing University, where Ya-Wen was studying music and voice. Hiao-Tsiun was Ya-Wen's music theory teacher. Hiao-Tsiun had returned to China after studying music for several years in Paris, France.

At that time, China was a dangerous place to be.

World War II had plunged most of the world into violence, and the Japanese were invading China. Hiao-Tsiun soon left the country and returned to Paris. He continued his studies and earned his Ph.D. in musicology, the study of music.

Ya-Wen had developed a crush on Hiao-Tsiun Ma. She was determined to go to Paris as soon as she got the chance. She returned to Hong Kong to earn money.[1]

World War II finally ended in 1945, but life in China did not improve much. The country was being torn apart by civil war. Communist rebels were trying to overthrow the weakened Chinese government. Ya-Wen left Hong Kong in 1949, when she was twenty-six.

She traveled with a friend from her college days: Tsiun-Cheng Ma, Hiao-Tsiun's sister. Tsiun-Cheng reintroduced Hiao-Tsiun and Ya-Wen to each other in Paris. The two musicians married on July 17, 1949, and Ya-Wen began using the name Marina Ma.

The couple's first child, a daughter, was born a little more than two years later, on July 28, 1951. Little Yeou-Cheng Ma soon showed a remarkable talent for music. She began playing piano and violin before she was three, and she made exceptional progress.

On October 7, 1955, Marina and Hiao-Tsiun Ma added a fourth member to their family. They named their newborn son Yo-Yo. The syllable *Yo* means "friendship." "With me," Yo-Yo later joked, "they seem to have got lazy and been unable to think of anything else, so they added another Yo."[2]

Yo-Yo soon proved every bit as talented as his older sister. He could sing in tune from a very early age, never singing too high or too low. He could hear

Yo-Yo's mother, Ya-Wen Lo, came from the island of Hong Kong.

when pitches made by voices or instruments were not quite right—even in music he had never heard before.

The Mas soon started their young son on piano and violin, like his sister. He did well on both instruments, but he did not seem to have much enthusiasm for the violin. His parents were puzzled until three-year-old Yo-Yo announced, "I don't like the sound violins make; I want a big instrument!"[3]

Dr. Ma waited a few months, thinking that Yo-Yo would change his mind. Yo-Yo kept nagging his father for his "big instrument." Finally, after Yo-Yo turned four, Dr. Ma gave in. He took Yo-Yo to an instrument shop, where Yo-Yo played a child-sized cello for the first time. The full name of the instrument is violoncello, but it is commonly shortened to just *cello*. "They couldn't find a chair small enough for me," Yo-Yo said later, "so I ended up sitting on three telephone books."[4] He was delighted.[5]

Now that Yo-Yo had chosen his instrument, Dr. Ma wasted no time in beginning his son's lessons. He taught Yo-Yo himself, using a method he had carefully worked out for teaching very young children. Yo-Yo had to memorize two measures of music a day. Each measure was only a few notes. He did not have to practice for very long—just ten minutes was often enough—but his father expected him to concentrate completely during that time.

As Yo-Yo's ability grew, Dr. Ma began teaching him one of Bach's solo cello suites using the two-measures-a-day method. He did this despite the fact that parts of the suites are hard to play even for professional cellists.

Dr. Ma's main instrument was violin, and soon he

decided it was time for his son to study with a real cello teacher. He chose Mme. Michelle Lepinte, a well-respected instructor. Mme. Lepinte was awed when the four-year-old played an entire Bach suite from memory.

By age five, Yo-Yo had learned three of the suites. Yo-Yo later said, "I found this [teaching] method ideal because I didn't like to work hard. . . . When a problem is complex, you become tense, but when you break it down into basic components you can approach each element without stress."[6] Yo-Yo would later use this "breaking it down into basic components" method during his solo career when he had to learn music in a short period of time.

Dr. Ma also tutored his children in French and in Chinese history and writing. They spoke Chinese at home and learned about their Chinese heritage and culture.

Although Yo-Yo worked hard at the cello, he was also very playful. He enjoyed singing songs, particularly one about frogs. He liked to jump around the room like a frog while he sang. And, like most younger brothers, Yo-Yo enjoyed tormenting his older sister. While she practiced piano, Yo-Yo would stand at the doorway and throw spitballs at her. Or he would crawl around at his sister's feet while she played. He liked to hold down the piano pedals so that Yeou-Cheng could not use them.

When Yo-Yo was five, he gave his first recital, at the Institute of Art and Archaeology at the University of Paris. He played one of the Bach suites he had so carefully learned, as well as other selections. He also played the piano. The audience applauded enthusiastically, and the concert was a great success.

Even though their son was very talented, Yo-Yo's parents decided not to overwhelm him with too many concerts. They limited his performances and continued his musical education.[7]

Still, Yo-Yo would soon find himself playing in another country. Before he was six years old, he and his sister gave several recitals in the United States. The first was in Rochester, New York, at Nazareth College. The Mas traveled there to visit Yo-Yo's uncle. The other recitals were in New York City. The Mas stayed there for several days before their return flight to Paris. The concerts were a success. Afterward, Dr. Ma was offered a position as director of music and children's orchestra conductor at the Trent School, a private elementary school in New York City. He accepted, even though the family had not planned to move to the United States. Dr. Ma had always wanted to conduct a children's orchestra.[8]

After returning to France for the summer, the Mas moved to New York City in the fall of 1962. Yo-Yo's parents wasted no time in finding a top-notch cello teacher for their son. He began studying with well-known cellist Janos Scholz. Scholz taught Yo-Yo for two years. He was impressed with the young boy's enthusiasm and talent. "He proved to be the most extraordinary, the most charming . . . little boy imaginable," he said. "He was so eager to acquire musical knowledge that he just lapped it up. . . . He was the ideal student, the student that a teacher always hopes for."[9]

It did not take long for the rest of the United States to discover just how talented the Mas were. Yo-Yo gave a private performance for famous cellist Pablo Casals in his home. Casals then contacted Leonard Bernstein, conductor of the New York Philharmonic. Bernstein was also a composer and an internationally known figure in the music world. The musical *West Side Story* is his most famous work.

Bernstein included Yo-Yo and Yeou-Cheng, who would accompany Yo-Yo on the piano, in a benefit concert in Washington, D.C., on November 29, 1962. President John F. Kennedy and his wife, Jacqueline, were in attendance. Yo-Yo, age seven, and Yeou-Cheng, age eleven, were the youngest performers on the program. They received excellent reviews. The concert was nationally televised as the *American Pageant of the Arts.*

Leonard Bernstein was not the only famous musician who helped jump-start Yo-Yo's career. Violinist Isaac Stern had seen Yo-Yo perform in Paris. Stern called Yo-Yo "one of the most extraordinary talents of this generation."[10] He kept track of the budding prodigy in New York. When Yo-Yo was nine, Stern arranged for him to study with Leonard Rose, a well-known cello player who also taught at the Juilliard School. Juilliard is one of the most prestigious music schools in the world. Yo-Yo entered the school's Pre-College Division, which holds classes on Saturdays.

In 1964, Yo-Yo's cello career hit several milestones. In February, he performed a cello concerto with the Doctors' Symphonic Orchestra—an amateur orchestra made up of doctors—in New York City. In a concerto, the cellist sits by himself in front of the orchestra. His part, called the solo part, is the highlight of the piece of music and is often very difficult. This was Yo-Yo's first appearance as a cello soloist with an orchestra.

The world-famous violinist Isaac Stern took a special interest in the talented young cellist.

He performed the Concerto No. 1 by French composer Camille Saint-Saëns (1835–1921). This piece is among the first concertos that cello students learn, because the part is not too hard. Later that year, the Ma children appeared on NBC-TV's *Tonight* show hosted by Johnny Carson.

In December 1964, Yo-Yo and Yeou-Cheng played in Carnegie Hall in New York City. They played a cello and piano duet called a sonata. They were among many performers in the concert, which was a benefit to help raise money for the school they were attending at that time, the École Française. Their performance was reviewed in *The New York Times*. Robert Sherman, the reviewer, was impressed by their performance. He wrote, "This is no children's piece, nor did they play it like children."[11]

Meanwhile, Yo-Yo and Yeou-Cheng went to school, just like other children their age. By the fifth grade, Yo-Yo was showing a rebellious streak. He began cutting classes. "I spent a lot of time wandering through the streets, mainly because I just wanted to be alone," he later explained.[12] Yo-Yo was confused. His Asian upbringing told him he should be obedient to his parents, quiet, and disciplined. His new American culture told him he should think for himself. "At home, I was to submerge my identity," Yo-Yo said. "You can't talk back to your parents—period. At school, I was expected to answer back, to reveal my individuality."[13]

In 1968, Yo-Yo switched to a different school, the Professional Children's School. He continued to skip classes, and eventually his teachers decided he must be bored. He was placed in an accelerated program so that he could graduate early.

At home, Yo-Yo's time was strictly managed. He practiced cello for a half hour before breakfast in the morning, then went to school. After school and a snack, Yo-Yo practiced cello for an hour, then did homework for at least two hours.

After dinner, Yo-Yo was allowed to watch television for a little while. His favorite programs were *Little House on the Prairie* and *Daniel Boone*. Then he spent more time on either homework or cello before going to bed. Later, Marina Ma said, "We didn't allow our children to have too many friends or to participate in too many outside activities. My Yo-Yo and Yeou-Cheng had no time for that."[14]

The Ma family's discipline was working wonders on Yo-Yo's cello playing. His skill was growing at a remarkable pace. His new teacher, Leonard Rose, was astounded not only by Yo-Yo's talent, but by how well the boy always prepared for his lessons.[15] "By the time Yo-Yo was eleven or twelve," Rose later said, "I had already taken him through the most difficult études [musical exercises]. He may have one of the greatest techniques of all time. I'm always floored by it."[16]

When Yo-Yo was thirteen years old, he gave his first concert on the West Coast. In 1968, the family flew out to visit Marina's sister in Berkeley, California. While they were there, Yo-Yo played the Saint-Saëns concerto with the San Francisco Little Symphony. Critic Arthur Bloomfield of the *San Francisco Examiner* described his playing as "flawless" and "staggering." After this triumph, requests for concerts flooded into the Ma household. The San Francisco Symphony, a top orchestra, invited Yo-Yo to return to California in two years to play the Saint-Saëns concerto with them.

Yo-Yo's parents continued to limit his appearances. They did not want to exhaust Yo-Yo, and they believed his education—both scholastic and musical—was of utmost importance. They also knew it was best not to let audiences have their fill of Yo-Yo's talent. It was better to whet people's appetite and leave them eager for more.[17]

From High School to Harvard

As Yo-Yo neared the end of his high school studies, his concert schedule grew busier. In March 1971, he performed a solo piece with the Harvard-Radcliffe orchestra in Cambridge, Massachusetts. Cambridge is across the Charles River from Boston. A month later, Yo-Yo returned to Cambridge to give a recital at Radcliffe College, the women's college affiliated with Harvard University. Yo-Yo visited Yeou-Cheng while he was there. She was studying biochemistry and music at Radcliffe. During the visit, Yo-Yo decided he liked Harvard.[1]

On May 6, 1971, Yo-Yo gave his first professional recital, called a debut, in New York's Carnegie Recital Hall. A twenty-one-year-old pianist named Emanuel Ax heard the recital. He later said, "I was completely bowled over. It seemed like the most perfect playing I had ever heard. . . . I remember saying, 'Someday I have to work with that person!'"[2] Ax would later become Yo-Yo's playing partner when the two formed the Ax-Ma duo in 1975.

After the recital, Leonard Rose decided it was time for Yo-Yo to start learning how to understand music on his own. He assigned him Beethoven's Fourth Sonata to learn without guidance. "He knew when to teach and when to let go," said Yo-Yo. "He gave me permission to work it out by myself."[3]

In June 1971, Yo-Yo graduated with his high school diploma from the Professional Children's School. He was only fifteen years old, and he felt he was not ready for a concert career.[4]

Luckily, Yo-Yo did not have to decide about his future right away. He spent the summer after high school graduation at a music camp called Meadowmount, in the Adirondack Mountains in Westport, New York. There, students spend seven weeks practicing, taking lessons, and playing chamber music. Chamber music is written for small groups of instruments in which each musician plays a different part.

This was the first time Yo-Yo had ever been away from home on his own. In his own words, he "went wild."[5] He skipped rehearsals, drank beer, and even left his cello outside in the rain. Yo-Yo felt confused about his identity. He was trying to figure out what he believed in and cared about.[6] That summer, Yo-Yo began to play the cello with much more emotion.

After Meadowmount, Yo-Yo knew he was still not

ready to be a professional musician. He also did not want to attend a conservatory, or music school, like Juilliard full-time.[7] In the fall, he enrolled at Columbia University in New York City. He continued to take lessons with Leonard Rose and classes at Juilliard, too. He soon dropped out of Columbia—without telling his parents.

Yo-Yo was also experimenting with alcohol. He obtained a fake I.D. card so he could buy alcoholic beverages, and he began drinking frequently with older friends. One day Ma got so drunk that he threw up in a practice room at Juilliard and passed out. He was rushed to the hospital, where doctors pumped his stomach. Because of this, he missed a rehearsal of the children's orchestra that his father conducted. His parents were deeply ashamed of his behavior. Fearing that he had set a bad example for Yo-Yo, Dr. Ma gave up his daily glass of wine before dinner. Yo-Yo felt embarrassed and guilty.[8] He stopped drinking after this incident.

During this difficult year, Yo-Yo was trying to decide whether he really wanted to become a musician. His experience during the summer of 1972 helped him decide. He attended the Marlboro Music Festival, a summer program in Marlboro, Vermont, for talented music students and young professionals. He spent hours there playing chamber music with other young, talented musicians. Sometimes they played until as late as 2:00 in the morning. Yo-Yo loved chamber music. "I thought there could be nothing better than to play string quartets [music for two violins, viola, and cello] for the rest of my life," he said.[9]

Here, at the Marlboro Music Festival, Yo-Yo is coached by cellist Mischa Schneider.

Yo-Yo was also inspired by Pablo Casals, revered as the world's greatest cellist in the first half of the twentieth century. "I didn't know I was definitely going to be a cellist; it was summers spent at Marlboro and other summer schools that were a tremendous inspiration to me," Yo-Yo later said. "To see someone like Casals stand up in front of the orchestra and scream at the top of his voice was catalytic [inspiring]. I thought that if [he] can feel that strongly about music at ninety-four then I can stick with this for the next 50 years."[10]

His first summer at Marlboro, Ma formed a close friendship with Jill Hornor, a violinist several years older than he was. She had just finished her sophomore year at Mount Holyoke, a women's college near Boston. Hornor was working in the office for the festival. "She was probably the first person who really wanted to find out what I truly thought," he said. "She used to say, 'What do you really mean by that?' That totally dumbfounded me."[11]

That summer, Yo-Yo finally decided what to do with the next few years of his life. He enrolled at Harvard. "Going there was part of finding out whether I could do anything else but play the cello," he later said.[12] Around that time, his family obtained a fine cello for him in a shop in France. The cello was made in 1722 by an Italian instrument maker named Matteo Goffriller, and it had been used by several famous cellists. Yo-Yo would eventually nickname it "Sweetie Pie."

Yo-Yo's playing was continually improving. "When he was about 17," said Leonard Rose, "he gave a performance of Schubert's *Arpeggione*, which is a holy terror for cellists, and it was so gorgeous I was moved to tears."[13] Yo-Yo began receiving invitations to play concertos. During his first year at Harvard, Yo-Yo had concerts almost every weekend, all over the world. The new popularity was too much for him. His grades were suffering. For the next three years, he limited his out-of-town engagements to one a month.

At Harvard, word about Yo-Yo's playing spread quickly. In his freshman year, one of his professors, Irven DeVore, heard him play a concert. DeVore was a classical music fan. The next day, Professor DeVore announced to the class that Yo-Yo's cello playing was better than that of the famous Pablo Casals. Yo-Yo was so embarrassed, he turned purple.[14]

Yo-Yo was soon playing many concerts in the Boston area. He performed concertos with Harvard's orchestras and the semi-professional Boston Philharmonic. He became very popular in Boston. Once, when a concert he was about to give was sold out, he sat in the lobby beforehand and played Bach suites for those unable to get in. Ma also volunteered to play all over Harvard's campus. He could be found playing cello nearly any-where, from dormitory common halls to Bach Society orchestra performances and productions of Gilbert and Sullivan (light opera).

All of this playing—and the practicing he had to do—made it hard for Yo-Yo to spend a lot of time study-ing. He was able to juggle his music career with his academic studies because, he said, "I was unbelievably lazy in everything. I had very low standards—I didn't feel compelled to get high grades, or to practice many hours every day."[15] Each semester, he picked one class

Before long, Yo-Yo was being compared with the great cellist Pablo Casals.

to work hard in. Otherwise, Yo-Yo often waited until the last minute to complete assignments, writing papers until late at night. Once, he even picked the lock of the music library so he could stay up all night listening to the music assigned for that semester. Occasionally, his bad study habits caught up with him. In his freshman year, Ma was placed on academic probation after sleeping through an exam. That meant that he could be forced to leave Harvard if his grades did not improve. Luckily, they did.

Yo-Yo was curious about many different subjects when he went to Harvard.[16] He picked a major called humanities. This let him take classes in a wide variety of subjects, including history, German, sociology, fine arts, and literature. He was interested in different cultures because of his multicultural upbringing: Chinese, French, and American. He wanted to study what made other cultures different and what they had in common.[17] One of his favorite classes was an anthropology class taught by Professor DeVore. "My whole life was in a sense changed by that course," said Yo-Yo.[18] DeVore's lectures interested Ma in the Bushmen of the Kalahari Desert in Africa. Later, Ma would travel to meet them.

Even though he was majoring in humanities, Yo-Yo took many music classes at Harvard. There was only one class that taught music performance. Most of the music classes concentrated on analyzing the theory behind how music is written. At first, Yo-Yo did not want to learn too much about music theory. He was afraid that thinking too much about how music is constructed would hurt his instincts for cello playing.[19] He had several professors, such as composers Leon Kirchner and Luise Vosgerchian, who encouraged and pushed him to learn to analyze music. Eventually, Yo-Yo became fascinated by what he was studying.[20]

Yo-Yo also learned quite a bit from the one performance class he took while at Harvard. It was a chamber music class taught by Leon Kirchner. Ma formed a piano trio with violinist Lynn Chang and pianist Richard Kogan. The three knew each other from Juilliard's Pre-College Division, and Yo-Yo had gone to Meadowmount with Chang. The young men spent hours working through the repertoire, or musical selections, for piano trio. Kogan was also Yo-Yo's roommate during his senior year at Harvard. The three musicians became good friends and continued to play together from time to time after graduation.

Harvard was not the only place Yo-Yo played chamber music during his college years. He continued to attend Marlboro every summer. In 1973, Ma's second year at Marlboro, he began playing with the pianist Emanuel Ax. They became close friends. Yo-Yo also met violinist Young Uck Kim at Marlboro. He would later join Yo-Yo and Emanuel to form a piano trio.

Even though Yo-Yo was very busy while he was at Harvard, he found time for one more commitment: his friendship with Jill Hornor. During Yo-Yo's freshman year, Jill went to Paris for a year of study abroad. The two began writing letters more and more frequently until each was writing a letter a day. Yo-Yo was accumulating hundreds of dollars in telephone bills with calls to Paris. At one point he even flew to Paris to spend a week with Jill. The next year, Jill returned to Mount Holyoke. After she graduated, she went to Cornell University, in Ithaca, New York, to do graduate studies in German literature. The two continued their long-distance relationship.

During the final year of his college career, 1976, Yo-Yo played for Mstislav Rostropovich. Rostropovich, considered the greatest living cellist, was at Harvard to give a master class. In a master class, students play before other students and an audience, then receive advice and criticism from the teacher as the audience watches. Yo-Yo played the first movement of the cello concerto by Czech composer Antonín Dvořák for Rostropovich. It was the same piece Rostropovich himself was playing that week with the Boston Symphony. Rostropovich was very critical of Yo-Yo because he knew Yo-Yo was very talented. He told him that his sound had no "center," meaning his playing was unfocused and lacked personality.[21] But by the end of the master class, the master cellist had offered to take Ma as a student.

In June 1976, Ma's Harvard years came to a close. He graduated with a bachelor of arts in humanities. Even though his grades were not the best, Yo-Yo felt that he got what he needed out of his time at Harvard. "Ultimately," he said, "the purpose of college is to open your mind to different things, to disciplines you don't know anything about. That purpose was served."[22] With his academic career behind him, it was time for Ma to begin his performing career.

An Emerging Star

As soon as he left Harvard, Ma dove right into a full-time performing career. From fall through spring, he played concertos and other solo pieces with orchestras all over the United States, and some in Europe as well. "At first I wanted to do everything, anything—London to L.A. and back to London," Ma said.[1] "All the traveling and concertizing seemed terribly exciting."[2] He spent his summers playing chamber music and teaching at music festivals, including the Spoleto Festival U.S.A. in Charleston, South Carolina; the Aspen Music Festival in Aspen, Colorado; and Tanglewood in Lenox, Massachusetts.

Even with an exhausting schedule, Ma tried to keep sight of his goal as a performer: to communicate with the audience. "I'd like to make [the] music live, come to life to the people coming from work, vacation, God knows what," explained Ma. "My goal is to have them concentrate. I can always tell, hear that special hush."[3]

Throughout all his traveling, Ma kept in close touch with Jill Hornor. By the spring of 1977, Yo-Yo and Jill had been dating for nearly five years. At that point, a friend advised Ma that it was time he made the relationship official. "If you don't do something," he said, "fish swim away."[4] Ma took his advice. After calling Jill to be sure she would be home, Ma bought a ring and two plane tickets to Cleveland, where Jill's parents lived. Then he dressed in a suit and tie, took a bus from New York City to Ithaca, and rang Jill's doorbell. When she answered the door, Ma knelt and asked her to marry him. Jill said, "Yes, sure!" The two then flew to Cleveland to share the happy news with her parents. Ma's parents, on the other hand, were not very happy at first. They had hoped their son would marry a Chinese woman. They worried that the couple's children would not learn Chinese traditions. Eventually they changed their minds and accepted Jill into the family.[5]

In April 1978, Ma gave a recital at New York's 92nd Street Y. The concert received a rave review from Joseph Horowitz, a critic for *The New York Times.* "Yo-Yo Ma . . . is a cellist of staggering ability," he wrote.[6] Ma was becoming well known.

A month later, on May 20, 1978, Yo-Yo and Jill were married. They soon moved into Harvard's Leverett House, where they would live for the next three years. Jill was a German tutor, and Yo-Yo was one of the university's artists in residence.

At first, Yo-Yo and Jill agreed to share the cooking and other household jobs. This did not work as they had planned. First of all, Ma said, "I've proved horrible at all domestic chores."[7] Second, Ma spent very little time at home. His career was taking off.

In addition to receiving excellent reviews for his concerts, in 1978 Ma also won a very prestigious award called the Avery Fisher Prize. The prize, awarded by New York's Lincoln Center, is given only to the most outstanding solo instrumentalists. Soon orchestras all over the world wanted Ma to perform with them. Every time Ma's agent called to offer him more concerts, he said yes. He did not think about how busy his schedule would become. For the first few years of his career, Ma played as many as 150 concerts a year. That is nearly one concert every other day.

Even though Ma played so many concerts, that did not mean he had to learn more than one hundred different pieces of music. Each year, he chose two or three concertos to play during the concert season. He picked these from the twenty to thirty concertos he had already learned. Ma also tried to learn several new pieces each year, music written by contemporary composers. He even commissioned, or requested, new works from composers. Ma felt it was important to play new music. "Modern music is now much more accessible than it used to be," he said. "I hope people get excited when a composer writes a new piece."[8]

Ma also wanted new pieces because there is not as much music for cello as there is for piano and violin, the most common solo instruments. "A pianist," said Emanuel Ax, "could go on playing for 100 years and not begin to play the complete standard repertoire [often-heard concert pieces]. For a cellist, if you are a talent like Yo-Yo, by the time you are twenty-five you have mastered all the cello concertos that are known."[9]

Violinist Isaac Stern gave Ma credit for expanding the cello repertoire. "Between Yo-Yo and Rostropovich," he said, "the amount of new music written for the cello in the twentieth century surpasses all the music written for cello in the past four centuries."[10]

In addition to his solo appearances, Ma continued to play chamber music as often as he could. He began performing regularly with pianist Emanuel Ax in 1975. They played about ten concerts a year together. Sometimes they spent more time talking than playing during their rehearsals. "For the first couple of years, we had long discussions," said Ma. "We'd argue and argue, and realize after two and a half hours that we were actually using different words to describe the same thing."[11] The two men paid careful attention to the music, trying to play it exactly as the composer intended.

Even though Ma was playing all over the world, he still found time to help out the college he had attended. In February 1980, he played with his old Harvard trio—violinist Lynn Chang and pianist Richard Kogan—to help raise money for a Harvard student service organization. He also played with the Harvard Chamber Orchestra, conducted by his former teacher Leon Kirchner.

In April 1980, Ma's career was threatened by a medical condition. He had a severe curvature of the spine, called scoliosis, and time was running out to fix it. Doctors were worried the curve would become worse and eventually cause his spine to squeeze his internal organs. He needed to have an operation, and it was somewhat risky. There was a small chance that nerves could be damaged, preventing Ma from playing the cello again. Ma understood the risk. "I used to think that life ended with that operation," Ma said. "I didn't dare plan ahead. I was prepared to do something else afterwards, there was always this one percent chance something might go wrong."[12]

Luckily, the operation was a success. It even made Ma stand two inches taller. For six months after the surgery, his upper body was enclosed in a cast that went up to his neck. The doctors cut the cast in a shape that would allow Ma to practice the cello. He joked that he liked the cast. "With my cast on, I felt like a football player," he said. "I had broad shoulders, a fabulous physique."[13] Ma gave a concert of the second Bach cello suite while he was still in the cast. Aside from that, Ma played very little during his recovery. "I didn't realize until after the operation," said Ma a few years later, "that I had been in constant pain. Now, knock on brain, I'll be able to play for many more years."[14]

After Ma's cast came off, he resumed his busy concert schedule. He and Emanuel Ax began occasionally playing piano trios with violinist Young Uck Kim. Their first appearance on the Boston University Celebrity Series, in 1980, was sold out. During the

1980–1981 concert season, Ma played about 120 concerts all over the world. Most were solos with orchestras.

Because Ma did so much traveling, he sometimes had to cope with unexpected situations. Once, when he was traveling on Germany's notoriously fast-paced Autobahn highway, his car's tire went flat. While he waited for help, he decided to make use of the time. Cars whizzing by on the Autobahn saw a strange sight by the side of the road. A young man was seated on a

Ma and pianist Emanuel Ax became friends and music partners. The third person in the photo is the page turner for the piano music.

suitcase by a car with a flat tire, playing Haydn on the cello. Ma was practicing for a concert in Frankfurt that night. "People couldn't believe what they were seeing," said Ma.[15]

Even though Ma was considered one of the best, if not the best, cellist in the world, he still depended on former teacher Leonard Rose for occasional help. In January 1981, Ma paid him a visit. He was unhappy with his bow arm. After a few hours, Rose suggested Ma make a slight change to the way he held the bow. "Suddenly everything clicked!" said Ma.[16]

In 1981 Ma continued to make time in his schedule for chamber music. A Beethoven recital Ma gave with Ax in Boston was so popular that the location had to be changed from a small recital hall to Symphony Hall, the large concert hall where the Boston Symphony plays.

That year Ma took on an additional challenge. He rewrote several violin pieces by the early-nineteenth-century composer and violinist Niccolò Paganini so that he could play them on the cello. These pieces were from Paganini's set of 24 Caprices, which are among the hardest pieces of music ever written for the violin. They would not become any easier on the cello. "I made myself do them for some perverse reason," said Ma. "A week before I was to play them, I panicked. I started practicing four hours a day and developed a new muscle on my hand. When I got to the concert I almost had to be pushed out on stage. But I did it—for which I'm now grateful. Everything else is easy compared to that."[17]

In July 1981, Ma played at the Kennedy Center in

Washington, D.C. First he and Ax played a Beethoven sonata. Then Ma took the stage with the Mostly Mozart Festival to play the D-major cello concerto by the eighteenth-century Austrian composer Franz Joseph Haydn (1732–1809). When he finished, the audience rose to give him a standing ovation. The orchestra's cello section even applauded. And just when the cheering began to die down, someone began clapping again, and Ma had to return to the stage for another bow. Apparently Ma still was not sure his performance was good enough. When he saw his uncle backstage, he asked, "Was it all right?"[18]

That fall, the Mas moved out of Leverett House into a home in Winchester, Massachusetts. Jill had to start packing without her husband, although he did take a week off from practicing to help finish the move. They did not spend much time there at first. During the 1981–1982 concert season, Jill took time off from teaching so she could join Yo-Yo on tour.

In 1983, Ma experienced several changes in his musical life. He bought an Italian cello made by Domenico Montagnana in 1733. Every instrument is unique, and Ma liked the "clarity" and "extraordinary dynamic range" of the Montagnana cello.[19] He also began a career as a recording artist. Among his first recordings were two of Beethoven's sonatas for cello and piano with Emanuel Ax, the Saint-Saëns and Lalo cello concertos with the National Orchestra of France, and the five Paganini caprices he had adapted. He was accompanied in the Paganini by pianist Patricia Zander, a longtime friend and collaborator. Ma also recorded his favorite music, the Bach cello suites, for the first time.

Ma was enjoying something new and exciting in his family life, too. He became a father when he and Jill had their first child, Nicholas. After Nicholas's birth, Ma made a list of priorities in his life. He wanted to make sure he always gave his best effort every time he played. "First of all, I promised myself that if I ever felt really burned out and lost enthusiasm for giving concerts I'd be responsible enough to quit. . . . Second, I decided that every concert I played—no matter where, no matter if the city was big or small—was going to be special."[20]

Ma began saying no to some concerts. He wanted to spend less time traveling. "Alone on tour you can get very self-centered," he said. "It's easy to think of nothing but music and planning. . . . It's important to get away from it. I'd like some vacation time, private time—to live some semblance of a good life."[21]

That would not happen in 1984, which was another very busy year. Ma and Ax recorded two more Beethoven cello sonatas, and Ma also recorded sonatas by Bach, cello concertos by twentieth-century Russian composers Dmitri Shostakovich and Dmitri Kabalevsky, and the Concerto in D Major by Franz Joseph Haydn. He experimented with jazz, making a recording of a suite for cello and jazz piano trio by contemporary composer Claude Bolling. He also won his first Grammy Award, for Best Classical Performance: Instrumental (without orchestra) for his recording of the Bach cello suites.

That year, Ma acquired another cello, the Davidoff Stradivarius, made in 1712. Stradivarius cellos and violins are considered to be the best in the world.

Before Ma began using it, the Davidoff Strad was played by English cello virtuoso Jacqueline du Pré. Du Pré was an extremely popular soloist for about a decade beginning in the early 1960s. A disease called multiple sclerosis cut her career and her life short.

Not everything that happened to Ma in 1984 was good. That year he faced the loss of one of the most important musicians in his life. Former teacher Leonard Rose died after an illness of several months. "Leonard Rose was much more than my teacher," said Ma. "He was my mentor and my friend."[22] Now Ma would have to look elsewhere for musical companionship and advice.

Yo-Yo Ma
Branches Out

Yo-Yo Ma knew he was too busy. His family was growing. A daughter, Emily, was born in 1985. Ma needed some tips on how to cope with his crazy schedule. Famous violinist Itzhak Perlman, who is very dedicated to his family, told Ma that he must set aside time to be with his family. Following Perlman's advice, Ma refused to play concerts on his children's birthdays. He also reserved the month of July as a vacation month to spend time with his wife and children.[1]

Even though Ma was now scheduling his time more carefully, he was still playing many concerts all over the world. He continued to play concertos with the world's best orchestras. Some of the concertos had been written hundreds of years ago, like those by

Violinist Itzhak Perlman told Ma how to balance his family life and career.

Haydn. Some audience favorites were romantic, lush concertos written in the nineteenth century by such composers as Antonín Dvořák and Robert Schumann. Some were from the twentieth century, including the concertos by American composer Samuel Barber and the British composers Edward Elgar and William Walton. Ma's recording of the Elgar and Walton cello concertos won the 1985 Grammy for Best Classical Performance: Instrumental (with orchestra). Ma also played brand-new concertos that were written upon request for him, including one by his former Harvard professor Leon Kirchner.

Even though Ma was busy playing concertos, he reserved time for chamber music. In 1985 he finally got his first chance as a professional to do something he had loved since his summers at the Marlboro Music Festival: play in a string quartet. He went on tour with violist Kim Kashkashian and violinists Gidon Kremer and Daniel Phillips. The quartet's specialty was playing the last pieces that composers had written before they died. "If we had to find a name for ourselves," said Ma, "it would have been 'The Quartet That Plays Only the Late Works.'"[2] The group later released recordings of Shostakovich's and Schubert's final string quartets.

Most of Ma's chamber music, though, was performed with pianist Emanuel Ax. Two of their recordings won Grammys: the cello sonatas by Johannes Brahms (1985) and the Beethoven Cello Sonata No. 4 (1986). A year later, the duo released a set of the complete Beethoven cello sonatas.

By the late 1980s, Ma was ready to try playing a completely different kind of music: jazz. After meeting jazz violinist Stephane Grappelli, Ma decided he wanted to work with him. The two men performed concerts together and recorded an album called *Anything Goes*. It featured arrangements of songs by famous jazz composer Cole Porter. Unlike most of Ma's other recordings, *Anything Goes* did not get very good reviews. Writer Ed Siegel of *The Boston Globe* later said, "His one attempt at jazz, 'Anything Goes' with Stephane Grappelli, was not a success because anything didn't."[3]

Jazz is different from classical music in many ways. One of the most important differences is that jazz performers make up, or improvise, some of the music during the performance. Jazz composers often write down only the main tune, then leave the rest up to the musicians. Classical musicians, on the other hand, play exactly what the composer wrote. The composer spells out every note from beginning to end. Ma was never trained to play jazz, but he did do a little bit of improvisation in his concerts with Grappelli. Ma did not try playing jazz very often after this. He enjoys listening to jazz, though. Among his favorite performers are Miles Davis, John Coltrane, and the Turtle Island String Quartet.

Meanwhile, Ma continued his partnership with Emanuel Ax. In 1990 the two went on tour. They played famous sonatas by Beethoven and Russian composers Sergei Rachmaninoff and Sergei Prokofiev. They also played a brand-new sonata written for them by contemporary American composer William Bolcom. After their performance at Avery Fisher Hall in May, critic Bernard Holland of *The New York Times* commented on how the friendship between the two men seemed to improve their music-making: "The two have played together for many years and it shows," Holland wrote. "[Their musical] phrases . . . have an unusual sense of mutual understanding. One looks for a less corny way to explain this musical relationship, but friendship seems the only apt one."[4]

There may have been another reason for their

excellent concerts besides just friendship, according to Ma. He said that after working together for so long, he and Ax had developed a kind of chamber music mental telepathy. "We . . . have a built-in understanding," he said. "We can look at each other during a performance and know exactly what the other person is thinking."[5]

Ax and Ma often added other players to their duo to make trios and quartets, including violinists Young Uck Kim and Isaac Stern and violinist/violist Jaime Laredo. In 1991, a recording of two Brahms piano quartets played by Ma, Ax, Stern, and Laredo won a Grammy for Best Chamber Music Performance.

In the early 1990s, Ma formed another partnership with a completely different kind of musician. Singer and conductor Bobby McFerrin invited Ma to participate in a concert McFerrin was directing in San Francisco. McFerrin is best known for his 1988 album *Simple Pleasures*, which featured the hit song "Don't Worry, Be Happy."

McFerrin was conducting Beethoven's Seventh Symphony to celebrate his fortieth birthday. He had met Ma a few years earlier at Tanglewood, at a concert celebrating Leonard Bernstein's seventieth birthday. McFerrin wanted to improvise something with Ma during the concert. When Ma explained that he did not improvise, McFerrin agreed to write something for voice and cello. He put it off until the day before the concert. Then, Ma said, "The day of the concert he changed everything."[6] The two ended up improvising together for twenty minutes. Ma said, "I'd never done this before and was shaking."[7]

Among all of these concerts and recording projects, Ma still found time to educate young people about music. To reach young audiences, Ma appeared in children's music shows produced at Tanglewood. These were shown on the BBC television channels in England and on the Arts & Entertainment cable channel in the United States. He also appeared on children's programs like *Sesame Street* and *Mr. Rogers' Neighborhood*, where he played part of a Bach cello suite.

Ma wanted to help young cellists improve their playing, even though he did not have time to teach cello students regularly.[8] Whenever his schedule would allow it, Ma stopped at universities and conservatories to give master classes.

At master classes, Ma spends about half an hour with each student. He lets each play his or her entire piece without interruption and praises the positive aspects of the performance before offering suggestions to improve weaknesses. He encourages students to relax and play as expressively as possible. Once, a boy struggling to play on a poor instrument was given the chance to play his piece on Ma's own cello.[9]

Ma is also interested in teaching all young musicians, not just those who play the cello. Much of his teaching and coaching has taken place in the summer at the Tanglewood Music Festival. He often coaches student chamber music groups. He also occasionally solos with Tanglewood's youth orchestra. Music journalist Edith Eisler commented on one performance: "He treated them with total respect, inspiring them to give their best . . . and they obviously adored him," she wrote.[10]

Ma helped teach children about music as a guest on Public Television's Mr. Rogers' Neighborhood *in 1985.*

Ma is often troubled by the training these hopeful young musicians receive in conservatories. Often, students are steered into practicing solo music and do not receive enough orchestra and chamber music playing experience. The top students are pushed to enter competitions. Music competitions are run like the Olympics. Judges watch and listen to the contestants play and give them scores. The highest-scoring participant wins.

Ma hates competitions. He thinks it is too difficult and arbitrary to use points to decide how well someone plays music. Also, he said, "The pressure on the nineteen-year-old who wins is enormous. This is their one big chance, and if they blow it because they're not ready, they're finished."[11] He thinks that older teens and young adults have more important things to do in life rather than just playing concerts. "I believe that the years between fifteen and twenty-something are the most essential to your development," he explained. "Everything you learn during that time is there for you to draw on for the rest of your life. If you put a lot into producing concerts instead of trying to open yourself to learning different ways of making music, you'll be a diminished person."[12]

The six Bach cello suites Ma had learned as a youngster remained an important part of his musical and personal life. In January 1991, he offered the suites to New York audiences in a new format: all in a row. In a marathon solo concert, Ma played all six Bach cello suites in one evening. Before he played, and during each intermission, he stretched and did deep breathing exercises to stay relaxed. He also ate very little. At 5 P.M., Ma began playing the first suite for a sellout crowd at Carnegie Hall in New York City. Four and a half hours after he began—including an hourlong dinner break and two intermissions—Ma played the last note of the sixth suite. The audience gave him a standing ovation.

After the concert, Ma went out with some friends to celebrate the performance. He returned at 3:00 in the morning to his wife's parents' apartment. They were asleep. The door was locked, and Ma realized that he had forgotten his keys. He did not want to wake anyone up by banging on the door, so he stretched out on the floor in the hallway and tried to sleep. It was not easy; maintenance men and newspaper delivery men were banging around in the elevator and in the halls, and it was very cold.

Ma's surprised in-laws found him outside their door at 6:30 in the morning, when they stepped out for the newspaper. Ma had to get up and get ready for an 8:00 A.M. appointment with Sony Classical, his record company. "That concert had meant so much to me," said Ma. "I had never tried something like that before and it was exhausting. And then three hours later, I'm a homeless person. That's the life of a musician."[13]

Later in 1991, Ma became involved in a project that took inspiration from one of Bach's cello suites and combined it with modern technology. He premiered a piece by composer and Massachusetts Institute of Technology (MIT) professor Tod Machover, written for hypercello. The hypercello was an attempt to unite technology and music. Ma played an electric cello that was outfitted with sensors and hooked up

Yo-Yo Ma and his sister, Yeou-Cheng, were just children the first time they performed at Carnegie Hall in New York City. Since then, Yo-Yo Ma has often packed the house at this famous concert hall.

to four computers. There were also sensors on the bow and on Ma's right wrist. It had taken a team of five people from the MIT Media Lab more than a year to assemble the hypercello and create software for it that could work as Machover intended.

The beginning of Machover's piece, called "Begin Again Again," is based on the sarabande movement from Bach's Second Cello Suite. The music came out different each time Ma played it. The computers reacted to the notes he played, how fast and loud he played them, and even what part of the bow he played them with. In the first movement, Ma used the electric cello. As the music begins, the cellist has a lot of control over what the computers do. But as the music continues, it gets faster and faster, with the computer music becoming wilder and wilder.

In the second movement, Ma played with the computers on his own, nonelectric cello. Then he listened to the sounds coming out of the computers and tried to play with them. This movement, which was a series of variations on a theme, was much slower. Each computer was attended by an engineer who manually triggered sounds that failed to go off automatically.

"Begin Again Again" was part of a recital at Tanglewood of works by American composers. Also on the program were Ma's arrangement for cello of Leonard Bernstein's Clarinet Sonata and a piano trio by Charles Ives. These two pieces would later appear on Ma's 1993 recording *Made in America*. Reviewers found Machover's music interesting but strange, even painful at times, because it became very high, fast, and loud until it hit a peak and became calm and quiet.

Later that month, the Bach suites would become even more meaningful to Ma. His father, who had first taught him the suites, suffered a severe stroke. It left him unable to walk or even sit up, and made speaking difficult. Before he died on August 28, 1991, Dr. Ma made one last request of his famous son: play Bach. Ma played the sarabande movement from the Fifth Suite for his father before he died. By then, Yo-Yo was also Dr. Ma. Harvard had awarded him an honorary doctorate in recognition of his remarkable career.

That same year, Ma received an invitation to approach Bach from a different perspective: as a speaker, not a performer. A friend asked him to speak at a meeting about Albert Schweitzer (1875–1965), a French musician, philosopher, and physician who was an expert on Bach. Ma was going to talk about Schweitzer's essays on Bach.

After Ma reread Schweitzer's essays and gave his speech at the meeting, he began to get an idea of a new way to experience Bach's music. Schweitzer said Bach was a "painterly" or "pictorial" composer, meaning that his music created visual images in the minds of those listening to it. Ma decided to make films about Bach's cello suites, working with other creative artists who were not musicians. He wanted to see how nonmusicians would interpret the suites.[14] The project would be called *Inspired by Bach*.

Ma hoped that these films would be shown on television and bring Bach to a new audience.[15] He approached Rhombus Media, a Canadian production company, about producing the films. He chose them because they specialized in films about the performing arts. Rhombus thought it was a great idea. "Three minutes into the meeting, we said, 'Let's do it,'" head producer Niv Fichman recalled.[16]

It would be years before the films were finished. Ma had no shortage of other projects during that time. In 1992, Ma and Bobby McFerrin teamed up in the recording studio to make a duet album called *Hush*. Several of the pieces on the CD are interpretations of classical pieces that showcase McFerrin's remarkable vocal abilities. Other pieces are folk tunes arranged by McFerrin or his original compositions. The CD sold very well, spending thirty-three weeks at the top of *Billboard* magazine's classical crossover chart. Several years later, the album would be certified as a gold record, meaning it had sold 500,000 copies.

Ma also played "Begin Again Again" several more times. The European premiere of the work was in Amsterdam, the Netherlands, in 1993. It took Machover's team from MIT Media Lab four days to get the complex hypercello system working in the Amsterdam concert hall, called the Concertgebouw. It was not ready until the night before the concert.

Ma saw Machover's hypercello piece as an interesting experiment. "I have two hopes for it," he said. "One is that it challenges us all to think about music and the development of possible instruments, and the other, more important one is that we get a good piece."[17]

Seeking New Musical Forms

Throughout nearly two decades of almost constant traveling and playing, Ma never stopped thinking about the Bushmen of the Kalahari Desert in Africa. He had learned about them in Professor DeVore's anthropology class at Harvard. "I'd always wanted to go see these people, this pre-agricultural, hunter-gatherer society," Ma recalled. "I was fascinated by them. . . . So I thought to myself, one day I am going to go there."[1]

That day finally came in 1993. With help from Professor DeVore, Ma assembled a film crew and a guide/translator and set off for Bushman villages in the African nation of Namibia. He planned to make a documentary of the trip.

Ma was astonished by how remote, how empty the

landscape was. "You see a lot of sky, and you don't see people for days," he said. "It's very scary."[2]

The Bushmen, also called the San, are a group of African people who have lived for centuries as hunters and gatherers. Their language is unique, as it features clicking sounds not heard in other languages. Many San still live in the traditional way, in small, mobile villages of about ten families that move around a large territory, gathering plants and fruit and hunting game. Other San, influenced by European culture, have settled into farming communities.

Ma brought his cello with him and played Bach for the Bushmen. They were not very interested. They

Meeting the Bushmen of the Kalahari Desert in Africa was a life-changing experience for Yo-Yo Ma.

wanted to play their music for him instead. Ma listened carefully to the villagers' music. He was fascinated by their homemade instruments, and he asked them many questions about how they worked. One instrument was made from the bows the Bushmen used to hunt. The player put the end of the bow in his mouth and hit the bowstring with his thumb and a stick. Another instrument, called the *gwashi*, was like a harp. It was made from natural materials, like wood, twigs, resin (tree sap), hide (dried animal skins), and sinew (strings made from animal tendons). Another instrument, called a *ventura*, is a little bit like a cello. It has one metal string, strung over an oil can. The bow is made from a twig. Ma tried to play the *ventura*. He found it difficult, and asked his translator to tell the Bushman *ventura* player he was much better at it. "Tell him the sound he makes is so much more beautiful," said Ma.[3]

The high point of the trip for Ma was an ancient Bushman ritual called the trance dance. He described it as a ritual that was a combination of "music, medicine, [and] religion."[4] The trance dance lasted all night. The women of the tribe sat around the fire, clapping and singing to a drumbeat. The men danced, and some went into a trance. The next day, Ma asked some of the women why they performed the trance dance. They told him it was because it gives them meaning.

Ma completed the documentary, called *Distant Echoes*, and returned to his professional life. The experiences he had in the Kalahari Desert stayed with him. "That was one of the most affecting trips or things that I've ever done in my life," said Ma. "There's hardly a week goes by I'm not thinking about that."[5] The trip redefined the role of a musician in society for Ma, and it would transform the rest of his music career. What he learned, he said, is that the purpose of a musician is "to uphold cultural memory, but also to innovate."[6] He decided that from then on, in addition to continuing his classical playing, he would try to learn and experiment with different kinds of music and cultures.

One of those experiments was the *Inspired by Bach* film project. Ma was working closely with Rhombus Media to choose different types of artists to interpret the cello suites for the camera. For the First Suite film, Ma picked Julie Moir Messervy, a garden designer. The Second Suite film would explore the field of architecture in virtual reality through the drawings of Italian architect Giovanni Battista Piranesi. Piranesi, who was born thirty-five years after Bach, had created drawings of imaginary prisons so strange that they could not be built. The Third Suite film was based on an art form with close ties to music: dance. Ma chose modern dance choreographer, or dance creator, Mark Morris for the project. Called *Falling Down Stairs*, the Third Suite film was the first produced. Rhombus and Ma began filming it in summer 1994.

The Fourth Suite film was just that: a film. It was directed by Atom Egoyan, a Canadian movie director. It was the only one of the six Bach films that was a fictional story rather than a documentary. It followed several characters whose lives were linked by Bach's music. Ma appears as himself in the film. For the Fifth

For The Music Garden *in the* Inspired by Bach *series, Ma played Bach's First Cello Suite. He invited a garden designer to create a garden using the music as inspiration.*

Suite film, Ma reached across the globe to Japan. He asked Kabuki actor Tamasaburo Bando to create a new Kabuki dance to the music. Kabuki is a traditional type of Japanese theater that features singing and dancing. The Sixth Suite film featured a different type of dancing: ice dancing. Jayne Torvill and Christopher Dean, the British ice-dancing champions, agreed to create a new routine to Bach's music.

The projects were not easy. Some ran into problems. For the First Suite film, Ma and Messervy wanted to show a music garden in Boston that would reflect Bach's music. Different areas of the garden would represent different parts of the suite. People visiting the garden would be able to push a button to hear a recording of the music. Ma and Messervy met with many politicians in Boston to try to persuade them to build the garden in time for the film's deadline. The plan failed because no one would donate enough money to begin the project. Luckily, the city of Toronto offered to host the garden. Construction was barely begun in time for the film. Instead of showing the garden, most of the First Suite film documented Ma and Messervy's struggle to persuade Boston to build the garden. The film ends with a ribbon-cutting ceremony at the park-in-progress in Toronto.

The Fifth Suite film project almost stopped before it began. In June 1994, Ma was flying from the United States to Tokyo to meet with Tamasaburo, director Niv Fichman, and the rest of the documentary team. During a layover in the Detroit airport, Ma received some bad news from Fichman. The project was over. Only hours before Fichman was to begin filming,

Ma wanted Bach's Fifth Cello Suite to be interpreted by Kabuki actors in Japan.

Tamasaburo had decided he did not want to do it. Ma was unwilling to give up. He went to Japan anyway. Once there, Ma managed to talk Tamasaburo into completing the film.[7]

Ma also continued to play concertos and chamber music after he returned from his Kalahari Desert trip, but he cut down his concerts to about seventy-five a year. At home, he enjoys doing small domestic chores that make him feel part of family life. "I take great pride in taking dishes out of the dishwasher; in waking up my children to go to school; and I absolutely love grocery shopping," he says.[8] To relax, Ma enjoys playing chamber music with close friends who are amateur musicians.

Even with a reduced concert schedule, Ma was still spending about half of his nights away from home. While he is away, he says, he thinks about his family "all the time."[9] He appreciates the effort his wife, Jill, has to go through to parent their two children when he is on the road so much. "She's really trying to do an incredible job in keeping us together. I think, in a way, that's the center of my life. . . . It . . . gives me the strength to go out and do what I do."[10]

Part of what Ma was doing was increasing his commitment to play new classical music. In 1994, he played works commissioned for him by American composers Christopher Rouse, John Harbison, Richard Danielpour, and John Williams. John Williams is best known for his movie music. He composed the soundtracks for the *Star Wars* and *Indiana Jones* films, *ET: The Extra-Terrestrial*, and many others.

That same year, Ma released a recording of

twentieth-century music. It was called the *New York Album* because all the pieces were composed in New York. One of the pieces, by composer Stephen Albert, was a new cello concerto commissioned for Ma by the Baltimore Symphony. The CD won a 1994 Grammy Award for Best Instrumental Solo Performance (with orchestra).

As for chamber music, Ma and Ax continued to collaborate. They played together at Tanglewood, and they recorded three clarinet trios with clarinetist Richard Stoltzman. The CD of the three trios, by Brahms, Beethoven, and Mozart, won a Grammy for Best Chamber Music Performance in 1995. It was Ma's tenth Grammy Award.

Meanwhile, Ma was pursuing another musical experiment. In 1994, he began rehearsing with fiddler Mark O'Connor and bass player Edgar Meyer. Ma wanted to explore the fiddling style of stringed instrument playing. Mark O'Connor is one of the world's best fiddle players, as well as an accomplished bluegrass guitar player. Ma had met him backstage at a concert at Carnegie Hall in honor of jazz violinist Stephane Grappelli's eightieth birthday. Edgar Meyer was working with O'Connor on bluegrass music at the time, but he is also a top-notch classical bass player.

Once the three men decided to work together, they began meeting about once a month to rehearse. It was difficult to coordinate their schedules, but they worked hard to find the time. "The rehearsals were very intense," said O'Connor. "Sometimes they would last more than 12 hours. We didn't have to do any of this, but we did it because we thought it mattered."[11]

Bassist Edgar Meyer and fiddler Mark O'Connor introduced Ma to the fiddling style of playing.

It took a year for Ma to learn how to match O'Connor's and Meyer's style of playing, including their rhythmic precision and style of bowing. Ma even changed the way he held the bow while he was playing fiddle music. Eventually, he got the hang of it. "We came up with some really great fiddle material that we hoped would challenge him," said O'Connor. "It was amazing to see him process this intellectually and make it work on his instrument. It has been quite a transformation."[12] The collaboration was a new experience for Ma. "I love being in a band," he said.[13] The trio began touring to packed concert halls in 1995 and released an album called *Appalachia Waltz* in 1996. The tunes on the recording were composed or arranged by Meyer or O'Connor. The CD spent twenty weeks at the top of Billboard's Classical Crossover chart in 1997, remaining on the chart for more than a year and a half, and gained positive reviews. Ma was proving that his crossover projects could be both commercial and artistic successes.

An Expanding Worldview

Even when Ma was playing well-known concertos with major orchestras, he still occasionally chose to do something a bit different. Most concertos are played in the first half of a concert, before intermission. After that, the soloist is usually finished for the night. But sometimes, instead of putting his cello away, Ma would sit in the back of the cello section and play in the orchestra for the second half of the concert. He particularly enjoyed doing this with the Philadelphia Orchestra. "It is an honor to play the back stands of the Philadelphia Orchestra," said Ma. "It's incredible the way those players listen, the knowledge they have. I admire it so much. And I feel the thrill of being part of something that's greater than the sum of its parts—being accepted as part of the team."[1]

In January 1996, Ma took center stage in an unusual concert series with the Philadelphia Orchestra. Most orchestra concerts contain only one concerto, and few orchestras plan concerts of only twentieth-century music. Ma and the Philadelphia Orchestra chose to defy both of those traditions. Ma played concerts made up entirely of three cello concertos written for him in the 1990s by Richard Danielpour, Leon Kirchner, and Christopher Rouse. Ma and the orchestra tried to help the audience feel comfortable with so much new music by talking to them about the music before each concert. Local reviewers were enthusiastic about the concerts, calling Ma's playing "superb."[2]

Not long after the concerts, Ma recorded all three pieces with the orchestra during a huge blizzard that dumped three feet of snow on Philadelphia. The weather did not chill the recording. The CD went on to grab two Grammy Awards in 1997.

Ma's successes made him very valuable to record companies. In spring 1996, Ma signed a five-year exclusive contract with his current company, Sony Classical.

Even though Ma was busy, he did not neglect music education. He continued to give master classes, and he even teamed up with trumpet player Wynton Marsalis to make a series of music-education videotapes. The four videotapes cover practicing, rhythm, musical forms, and jazz. A critic with the *Toronto Star* said Ma "steals the music-education

Ma and jazz trumpeter Wynton Marsalis made four videotapes to teach students about different aspects of music.

series away from the motor-mouth trumpeter."[3] Ma has even occasionally visited public schools, as he did after a concert with the Baltimore Symphony in November 1997.

Yo-Yo is not the only Ma to carry on the family tradition of promoting the music education that was so important to his father. His sister, Yeou-Cheng, is the executive director of the Children's Orchestra Society, founded by their father shortly after the family moved to New York City. She and her husband, classical guitarist and conductor Michael Dadnap, revived the orchestra society after it had lapsed for several years. The society runs four youth orchestras, a chamber music program, and private lessons for talented, motivated children.

Yeou-Cheng Ma's life is just as hectic as that of her more famous brother. She juggles her responsibilities as executive director with her work as a pediatrician for the Albert Einstein College of Medicine in New York City, where she treats children with developmental disorders. She also continues to play the violin as a chamber musician.

As he traveled to many different countries, Yo-Yo Ma could not help noticing that musical traditions and instruments seemed linked all over the world. In a museum in Japan, Ma saw a *biwa*—a pear-shaped stringed instrument—from the eighth century decorated with designs from Persia (modern-day Iran) and Central Asia. He realized that European stringed instruments like the cello had probably evolved from ancient Arabian and Chinese stringed instruments.

Yo-Yo Ma's sister runs the Children's Orchestra Society. Yeou-Cheng, center, poses with some of her students and faculty members.

By the mid-1990s, Ma was beginning to explore Asian, or "Eastern," music and how musical traditions in different geographic regions are linked.[4]

By 1997, Ma had become involved with several projects that explored traditional Chinese music. In his first major film project, Ma was featured on the soundtrack of the movie *Seven Years in Tibet*. The movie stars actor Brad Pitt as an Austrian mountain climber who journeys to Tibet during World War II. Although written by American composer John Williams, much of the music had an Eastern flavor.

Ma also collaborated with several composers of Chinese origin. In February 1997, Ma premiered *Spring Dreams*. It was written by Chinese-American composer

Bright Sheng, a University of Michigan professor. Unlike most cello concertos, *Spring Dreams* was not written for a typical European/American orchestra. Instead, Ma was accompanied by the National Traditional Orchestra of China. Founded in 1960, the orchestra contains only traditional Chinese instruments. Although *Spring Dreams* was structured like a piece of Western classical music—in two movements— its melodies sounded very Chinese.

Ma's second collaboration with a Chinese composer took place in view of the entire world. He was a featured soloist in *Symphony 1997 (Heaven Earth Mankind)* by Tan Dun. The piece was commissioned to celebrate the return of Hong Kong to China after 150 years of British occupation. Dun wrote it for solo cello, Western-style orchestra, children's choir, and replicas of ancient Chinese bells. It was performed during the ceremony turning Hong Kong over to the Chinese, which was broadcast internationally. Sony Classical, Ma's record company, released a CD of the piece later that year.

Ma's search for new kinds of music to play also took him to Buenos Aires, the capital of Argentina. He was investigating the tango, a dance form invented in Argentina. He was particularly interested in the tango music of twentieth-century Argentine composer Astor Piazzolla. Piazzolla had taken traditional Argentine tango music and fused it with elements of classical music and jazz. He created a new kind of tango that was meant more for listening to in concert halls than for dancing to in clubs and bars. Piazzolla's music was not always popular in Argentina. Some people did not like it because it was different from traditional tango. "Did you know that Astor Piazzolla got death threats?" Ma once asked. "People called and said: 'If you write another piece like that, you're dead.' I love that. Imagine people caring so much about music!"[5]

After months of reading Argentine books, studying Piazzolla's music, practicing, and rehearsing, Ma participated in two tango-related recordings, which were released in 1997. One was the soundtrack to a movie called *The Tango Lesson*, about a romance between a British film director and her Argentine tango instructor. Ma contributed a version of the Piazzolla piece "Libertango" to one track of the CD.

Ma also made a full-length CD of Piazzolla's music, called *Soul of the Tango*. He collaborated with some of the world's top tango players to make the recording. The CD featured a duet between Ma and Piazzolla playing the *bandoneon*, an Argentine accordion—even though Piazzolla died in 1992. Ma was playing along with a Piazzolla recording from 1987. *Soul of the Tango* won the Grammy for Best Classical Crossover Album in 1998.

On December 4, 1997, Ma and an ensemble featuring piano, *bandoneon*, violin, guitar, and bass kicked off a tour of tango music in Seattle. The tour included appearances in Washington, D.C., New York, and Baltimore. Later, Ma wrote the foreword to a book about Astor Piazzolla called *Le Grand Tango*.

Meanwhile, Ma was still busy with other projects. In 1997, the *Inspired by Bach* films were finally released to the public at their world premiere in Canada. In 1998, Lincoln Center in New York City featured Ma in its

Great Performers series, sponsoring several concerts and events for him. Ma showcased his tango skills in a Piazzolla concert, and he also played two modern works for cello and orchestra. One was *Symphony 1997* by Tan Dun. The other was *The Protecting Veil* by John Tavener. Later that year, Ma would play *The Protecting Veil* with the Los Angeles Chamber Orchestra and release a CD of the work, recorded with the Baltimore Symphony Orchestra. The piece was inspired by the composer's Russian Orthodox Christian religion. It was slow and quiet, like a musical meditation.

The main focus of the Great Performers series was Ma's interpretations of the Bach cello suites. Lincoln Center screened the six *Inspired by Bach* films in March 1998, before their appearance on American public television in April 1998. The Great Performers series also sponsored a marathon concert of the cello suites at the Church of St. Ignatius Loyola in Manhattan. As he had in 1991 and several times since then, Ma performed all six Bach cello suites in one day. In *The New York Times*, critic James Oestreich praised the music and Ma's performance, saying, "The cello suites, in the hands of a master, can seem the grandest . . . of statements . . . Mr. Ma's technical command was complete, as usual. . . . This venture proved a notable success."[6]

Ma's films of the Bach suites did not receive the same praise as his live performances of Bach's music. Critical reaction to the films was mixed. Most critics liked *Falling Down Stairs*, the film of the Third Suite featuring the Mark Morris Dance Troupe. Some critics praised the films featuring Kabuki and ice dancing (the Fifth and Sixth Suite films), but most thought the other films were "a more uneven lot," as one critic said.[7] Even Ma's friends were critical. One of his former college professors, Leon Kirchner, said the films were "baloney, unworthy of a supreme musician like Yo-Yo. I told him he should have saved a suite for Tiger Woods."[8]

Opinions were quite different about the new recording of all six Bach suites that Ma released along with the films. Critic Terry Teachout called them "a major musical achievement . . . a distinct improvement on the version he recorded at the age of 26."[9] Critic David Patrick Stearns wrote, "The recordings provide ample evidence that America's finest cellist is getting even better."[10]

Even with negative reviews of the *Inspired by Bach* films hitting the papers at the end of March 1998, Ma did not lose his sense of humor. On April 1, 1998, Ma told an interviewer for National Public Radio (NPR) he was going to give up the cello to play the *bandoneon*. NPR even aired a recording of Ma playing a movement of a cello suite on the Argentine instrument. Upset listeners called radio stations to complain about Ma's abandonment of his lifelong instrument. NPR and Ma had only one reply: "April Fool!" Those listeners had not realized that the report was just an April Fool's joke.[11]

Traveling the
Silk Road

Eventually, Ma began focusing his international music interests on one geographic area: the Silk Road. The Silk Road is not a highway, or even a real road. The name refers to a network of ancient trade routes that linked Asia and Europe from 500 B.C. to about A.D. 1500. Before Europeans and Asians discovered reliable ways to import and export goods by sea, trade routes for silk, spices, and other goods flowed over land. The Silk Road stretched from cities on the Mediterranean Sea through Central Asia and on to China, Korea, and Japan. Ma decided he wanted to bring Western and Eastern musicians together to explore how their traditions had influenced each other hundreds of years ago.[1]

Ma began talking to friends and colleagues about his ideas. Then, in 1998, he founded the Silk Road Project. At first, he organized conferences about the Silk Road. During a conference in Paris in June, Ma met Theodore Levin, an ethnomusicologist and professor at Dartmouth College. An ethnomusicologist studies music in relationship to culture. Levin had spent twenty-five years traveling in Central Asia and studying the region's traditional music. He wrote a book about his experiences called *The Hundred Thousand Fools of God: Musical Travels in Central Asia.*

Ma and Levin decided to work together. Ma would be artistic director of the Silk Road Project—in charge of directing musical activities—and Levin would be the curatorial director. It would be Levin's job to coordinate all of the project's activities. Levin took a leave of absence from Dartmouth to head the project.

Ma had much bigger plans than just learning about shared musical history. He wanted to organize collaborations between Western (American and European) and Eastern (Asian) musicians that would result in new music based on multiple musical traditions. He also wanted to bring attention to the musical traditions of non-Western countries. He and Levin were concerned that some traditions could be lost as popular Western culture invaded more and more parts of the globe.

Sony Classical provided the initial funding to get the project started. Dr. Levin and others traveled to Eastern Europe and Asia, seeking composers and musicians who would be willing and able to work with Westerners.

A man travels with his camel over part of the Silk Road. This network of ancient trade routes stretches from Asia to Europe.

At the same time, Ma had not stopped thinking about Bach. He had begun playing Bach's music differently. He was influenced by a growing movement within classical music to try to play pieces as they had been performed when they were written.[2] He began tuning his cello slightly lower when he played Bach. This was closer to the tuning of Bach's time. Ma held his bow a bit differently, too, with his hand higher up the stick. He was also influenced by what he had learned about fiddling by working with Mark O'Connor and Edgar Meyer on *Appalachia Waltz*. He felt that the fiddling style of playing was close to the music of Bach's time, called Baroque.[3]

Eventually, Ma decided he wanted to experiment more with playing Baroque music in a more authentic way. He decided he wanted to use a "period" instrument, which is an instrument built or changed to imitate the instruments of a certain time period. Ma chose to alter his Stradivarius cello—which was originally built during the Baroque period—to make it more closely resemble its original form. He removed the endpin, a metal post at the bottom of the cello that sticks into the floor. This forced him to grip the cello between his knees. He also changed his strings from modern metal to old-fashioned gut. Instrument

Ma performs with two members of the Silk Road Ensemble.

makers in London and Paris flattened the bridge—the piece of carved, curved wood that holds up the strings—and changed the tailpiece, which anchors the strings at the base of the cello. These changes reduced the pressure on the body and neck of the instrument. Ma played the refitted cello with a Baroque bow, which is lighter and has a different curve from a modern bow. Players cannot play as loud using Baroque-style instruments and bows.

The initial transition was difficult, said Ma. "Gut strings are unreliable. . . . They squeak and squawk at times, and they constantly go out of tune. But what I learned is that with less volume, the experience is more private, more intimate. Playing with less tension encourages you to think, to reflect more. It's extremely pleasurable."[4]

Ma's first recording on the changed instrument, *Simply Baroque*, was released in January 1999. He made the recording with the Amsterdam Baroque Orchestra, which uses period instruments.

Not everyone enjoyed Ma's Baroque experiment as much as he did. Some critics did not think he was very good at playing cello in the Baroque style. After Ma played a concert in London in April 1999, critic Helen Wallace of the London *Times* wrote, "There is more to playing a gut-strung cello with a Baroque bow than getting the equipment right." She criticized his tone, saying it sounded "squeezed," and said he did not play the notes in tune.[5]

Even though he received mixed reviews, Ma decided to leave his Stradivarius in its Baroque setup indefinitely. "The repertoire is so rich and beautiful, I want to continue to play it," he said.[6] He would record a sequel to his Baroque CD, called *Simply Baroque II*, the following year. The Bach cello suites were not included on either Baroque recording. Ma continued to play them on his Montagnana cello instead of the altered Stradivarius.

Even with a variety of unusual projects making demands on his time, Ma was still able to deliver top-notch performances of standard cello concertos. His summer 1999 performance of concertos by Haydn and Schumann with the Chicago Symphony was very well received.

A few months later, Ma could be found at his regular summer retreat: Tanglewood, one of his favorite places. "Maybe it's the hills," he once said, "but I get so calm and psyched when I get close to Tanglewood."[7]

While there, Ma gave master classes and played chamber music with Emanuel Ax. He also played in *Don Quixote* with an orchestra of young American and German musicians. *Don Quixote,* by Richard Strauss, is not a cello concerto, even though there is an important solo cello part. It is a tone poem—a piece written to tell a story. Strauss's music tells the famous story of Don Quixote, the title character of the book by Spanish writer Miguel de Cervantes. In the piece, the solo cello represents Don Quixote himself. His companion, Sancho Panza, is played by a solo viola.

Shortly after leaving Tanglewood, Ma flew to Weimar, Germany. He and the conductor of the Chicago Symphony, Daniel Barenboim, were starting a youth orchestra called the West-Eastern Divan Orchestra in hopes of encouraging peace in the Middle East. The one hundred student musicians in the group were from Middle Eastern countries such as Israel, Egypt, Syria, and Iraq.

Ma also worked with American young people— through television. In fall 1999, he appeared on the season opener of the hit animated children's program *Arthur* as a large, cello-playing gray rabbit with glasses. He and a hot young jazz saxophonist named Josh Redman performed in the episode, called "My Music Rules." The theme of the episode was that children should feel that it is okay to like more than one kind of music.

Meanwhile, Ma was still hard at work on the Silk Road Project. By 1999, he had assembled a panel to look at the work of forty composers from Central Asia and Eastern Asia. The panel chose sixteen composers to participate in the project and commissioned a new work from each of them. The composers' countries included Azerbaijan, Tajikistan, Uzbekistan, China, Mongolia, and Iran. Ma was also working to find additional funding for the project. He would eventually secure financial support from large corporate sponsors like Siemens, Inc., and the Ford Motor Company, as well as the Aga Khan Trust for Culture, a nonprofit foundation dedicated to supporting traditional culture in Central Asia.

Among the first activities of the Silk Road Project was an album by Ma of solo cello music. Most of the music on the CD reflects the influences of Eastern music. One piece, called *Seven Tunes Heard in China,* was composed by Bright Sheng. Sheng is a consultant to the Silk Road Project. The two men had worked together before on *Spring Dreams* in 1997. It also included a piece by Mark O'Connor, *Appalachia Waltz*, representing fiddling traditions that traveled from Europe and Asia, and a piece by Hungarian composer Zoltan Kodaly. The Sonata for Solo Cello by Kodaly is the only standard classical work on the CD and is the longest and most intense. It is thirty-five minutes long and one of the more difficult pieces in the cello repertoire.

Ma also performed these pieces on a tour of solo concerts. In the fourth movement of Bright Sheng's piece, called "The Drunken Fisherman," Ma had to pluck and strum his strings instead of using the bow. Most of the time, cello players pluck the strings with the fingers or thumb of their right hand. Sheng's piece required a different technique. The tune was originally performed in China on a seven-stringed plucked instrument like a guitar.

To make the cello sound more like a guitar, Ma needed a pick. He decided to use the key card from his hotel room as a pick after discovering that it created the perfect sound. He also played *The Cellist of Sarajevo* by David Wilde and Kodaly's Sonata for Solo Cello. A reviewer for *The Washington Post* wrote, "Only an artist with the charm, charisma and celebrity of Yo-Yo Ma could have sold out the Kennedy Center Concert Hall . . . for a program so defiantly uncompromising as the one the cellist played there late Saturday afternoon. Yet Ma . . . not only kept audience members in their seats through the challenging concert, he also left them cheering at the end."[8]

Ma played the same program in London. The critic for the London *Guardian* praised Ma's performance: "Ma's performance of the Kodaly sonata . . . is a tour de force that has you on the edge of your seat. . . . A standing ovation followed."[9] Afterward, Ma played Bach suites as an encore. He let the audience call out numbers between one and six to request a specific suite.

All these projects kept Ma very busy, and busy people can sometimes be forgetful. In October 1999, Ma made headlines when he accidentally left his Montagnana cello in a New York taxicab. He was on his way to his hotel after visiting Isaac Stern, and planned to meet his wife to take her to dinner. Ma was a little surprised by how much press attention this received. He said, "I can play concerts for years and years and years, and you know, some people will say, 'How very nice. Nice playing. Thank you very much.' But you lose one cello in a taxicab, everybody knows about it! [They give you] the knowing look: 'Oh. Hi. Been in a taxi lately?'"[10]

Luckily, Ma had saved his cab receipt. Police were able to track down the cab and driver in only a few hours. The cab was in a garage in Queens, New York. The cab driver did not even realize the $2.5 million cello was still in his trunk. Ma was very relieved to get the priceless instrument back. "Somehow magic happened, and I have my cello," he said. "The instrument is my voice, so I need it. . . . [Otherwise] I would be crying right now."[11]

"Been in a taxi lately?" Ma was very happy to be reunited with his 266-year-old cello.

9

When Strangers Meet

By summer 2000, the Silk Road Project was ready to begin the next step: preparing for performance. Ma organized a twelve-day workshop at Tanglewood. He and Levin invited about sixty musicians from all over the world to meet there and rehearse. They were trying out the new pieces of music that had been composed for the project. With so many different countries represented, the musicians had to have translators so they could talk to each other. Most of the musicians were from countries like Mongolia, China, and Iran—although some already made their homes in the United States—but some were Americans or Europeans trained in classical music. Like Ma himself, these classical players were eager to experiment with playing Eastern-style music.[1]

Ma did not stop at playing Silk Road–inspired pieces on his cello. He learned to play a new instrument, the *morin khuur*, also called the Mongolian horse-head fiddle. The top of the neck of the instrument, called the scroll, is carved like a horse's head. It has two strings. One of the reasons Ma was interested in the fiddle is that his family name, Ma, means "horse." Ma felt that the style of playing used for the horse-head fiddle was similar to Baroque cello and Western fiddle playing. "Take away all the technological developments," Ma said, "and you find the point, maybe 500 years ago, where all the musical traditions converse with each other."[2]

Ma's involvement with the Silk Road Project also led him to another film project. He played on the soundtrack of the movie *Crouching Tiger, Hidden Dragon*, directed by Ang Lee. The music was by Tan Dun, who also composed *Symphony 1997*. The score was written for a Western orchestra and Asian instruments. Dun was trying to make music that sounded like a blend of Western and Eastern

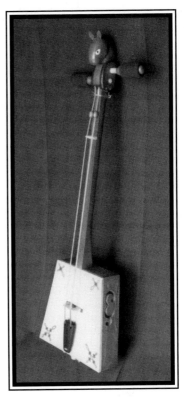

Playing the morin khuur, *or Mongolian horse-head fiddle, was similar to Western fiddle playing.*

musical traditions.[3] To get a feel for the music, Ma watched scenes from the movie. He recorded his part without hearing the accompanying orchestra parts. The soundtrack was nominated for an Oscar and won for Best Original Score. Ma performed excerpts at the Oscar ceremony.

Ma's new commitment to exploring Central and East Asian music did not stop him from continuing to dedicate time to education. In June 2000, Ma was a guest artist at the World Cello Congress held at Towson University outside Baltimore, Maryland. He gave several master classes, including one for very

Ma and Itzak Perlman performed at the Academy Awards ceremony, March 2001, when composer Tan Dun won an Academy Award for the soundtrack to Crouching Tiger, Hidden Dragon.

young cellists. In that class, two groups of four cellists each played chamber music for Ma. The students' teacher, John Kaboff, was impressed by the results Ma drew from the young musicians. "I was really amazed at how their playing level rose," he said. "The kids learned to use their eyes and ears in a way that made them sound much more musical and together."[4]

Ma also managed to find time to make music with old friends. In December 2000, he and Emanuel Ax reunited for a duo tour to celebrate their twenty-fifth year of playing together. They played sonatas by Brahms and Mendelssohn, among other works. Ma also spent more time with Edgar Meyer and Mark O'Connor. The trio teamed up with bluegrass singer Alison Krauss and folk-pop singer-songwriter James Taylor for a sequel to *Appalachia Waltz* called *Appalachian Journey*. The musicians went on tour to support the album, which won a Grammy Award for Best Classical Crossover Album in 2000. Sony also released a video recording of a live performance by the group.

Near Christmas 2000, Ma tried out a new career: acting. He appeared as himself on an episode of the popular television drama *The West Wing*. He played an excerpt from Bach's First Cello Suite as a guest performer during a White House Christmas party.

At the beginning of the new year, the Silk Road Project expanded its efforts to include more music and more countries. A panel reviewed the work of composers from Armenia, Italy, India, Japan, Korea, Pakistan, and Turkey. They picked four more composers to create new musical works.

The project was scheduled to begin performances

Martin Sheen, as the United States president, welcomed Yo-Yo Ma to the White House on an episode of the television drama The West Wing.

in August 2001. Before that tour began, New York audiences had an opportunity to enjoy a preview of some Silk Road music. In March 2001, Ma premiered two works inspired by the project with the New York Philharmonic. One was specifically commissioned for the project. It was by Iranian composer Kayhan Kalhor, called "Blue as the Turquoise Night of Neyshabur." The piece was written for six Western stringed instruments, plus Ma on cello, with parts for *kamancheh* (Persian spiked fiddle) and three other Persian instruments. Kalhor, a *kamancheh* virtuoso, played the part himself. He also played with Ma on the other premiere on the program. This was a work for cello by Richard Danielpour entitled "Through the Ancient Valley." It was Danielpour's second cello work for Ma. This time, Danielpour drew on his Iranian heritage to lend the piece an Eastern flavor, including a part for *kamancheh*, played offstage. The program finished with a performance of a standard classical work written with Central Asia and the Middle East in mind: *Scheherazade* by Nikolai Andreyevich Rimsky-Korsakov. The piece, written in 1888, was inspired by the collection of Arabian folk tales called *One Thousand and One Arabian Nights*.

Just before leaving for their tour, the Silk Road Ensemble gathered in France for a week of rehearsals. Ma was pleased with how well the group worked together. "What's impressive about this group is that there are so many leaders, so many people who can take charge," said Ma. "Everybody takes a leadership role in something. None of us knows everything about everything, but when we pool our resources we have a pretty incredible knowledge base."[5]

The musicians in the ensemble were just as pleased with Ma. Kayhan Kalhor said, "As I've gotten to know Yo-Yo, I've come to admire not only his energetic, charismatic musicianship but his character. He creates this positive energy wherever he is, and that's a rare person, anywhere."[6]

The Silk Road Project's 2001–2002 tour was planned as a cooperation with partner cities. Each city hosted a multiday festival of performances, lectures, and workshops. The first Partner City Festival took place at the Schleswig-Holstein Music Festival in

Germany. It had been moved there after plans to begin the tour in Salzburg, Austria, had fallen through.

The weeklong festival showcased the new music that had been commissioned for the Silk Road Project, as well as traditional music from Central and East Asia, performed on traditional instruments. Each concert also featured a piece of "standard" classical music that had been influenced by Eastern music. These pieces included works such as piano trios by Ravel and Shostakovich, the Debussy Cello Sonata, and the Kodaly Sonata for Solo Cello. All these pieces were written within the last 150 years. Each of the Silk Road Ensemble's concerts throughout its tour would follow this format.

Audiences and critics alike were fascinated. "In one Silk Road concert in Germany I worried about whether I had given enough information in introducing a singer from a very different cultural background," said Ma. "But the audience just burst into wild applause at the end, and I didn't really need to explain anything."[7] Performances of Mongolian long-song by this singer, Khongorzul Ganbaatar, were very popular. Mongolian long-song requires a singer to sing for a very long time without taking any breaths. The music also goes very high. One critic described Ganbaatar's voice as "exhilaratingly unearthly."[8] Another said her solo performance was "absolutely arresting. . . . She had the audience of about 1,000 pounding the stableboards."[9] (The performance took place in the riding ring of a horse stable.)

Part of Ma's goal in creating the Silk Road Project was to bring different cultures together and to show the positive things that can happen, as he often says, "when strangers meet."[10] Unfortunately, not long after the Silk Road Ensemble's performances in Germany, cultural hatred grabbed headlines. On September 11, 2001, terrorists crashed planes into the World Trade Center in New York City and the Pentagon in Washington, D.C., killing thousands of people. Ma thought about canceling the Silk Road Project but decided not to. "There was a need for people to be together," he said.[11] Although concerns about security forced the Silk Road Project to cancel its planned fall tour to Central Asia, it added stops in Dallas and Atlanta. Ma and Levin planned to reschedule the Central Asia tour at a later date.[12]

The Silk Road Ensemble continued its tour without the Central Asian dates. The next stop was Washington, D.C., in October 2001, followed by Japan in December, Europe in April 2002, then California, New York, and Seattle, Washington.

After the concert in Washington, D.C., a critic for *The Washington Post* expressed concern that the Silk Road Ensemble's concerts would be difficult for audiences to appreciate. "Cellist Yo-Yo Ma has produced a concert that will probably divide audiences and critics alike. His Silk Road Project . . . is a risk for him . . . because it is devoted to sounds with limited easy-listening potential."[13]

The critic need not have worried. In Seattle, for example, audiences—and critics—loved the Silk Road Festival. Reviewer Melinda Bargreen wrote, "Each night's concert was met with the kind of roars more commonly heard in a football stadium, as the artists were brought back again and again for spontaneous encores before an audience that just wouldn't let them leave the stage."[14] The enthusiasm for the music carried over, leading to more concerts of Silk Road–style music in local concert venues and in schools.

This sparking of local interest in Asian music is part of the mission of the Silk Road Project. In addition to concerts by the Silk Road Ensemble, the project sponsors lectures, workshops, and outreach in each partner city. It offers a Web site (http://www.silkroadproject .org) and an educational program called Silk Road Encounters. The project also published a book in conjunction with the Smithsonian Institution's Sackler Gallery. It is called *Along the Silk Road* and includes a conversation between Ma and Levin.

The Silk Road Project's cooperation with the Smithsonian Institution went much deeper than publishing a book. The final stop on the first Silk Road Ensemble tour was in Washington, D.C., in June and July 2002. There it became part of the Smithsonian Folklife Festival. In conjunction with the Silk Road Project, the theme of the festival was "The Silk Road: Connecting Cultures, Creating Trust." It was the first time in the history of the annual Smithsonian Festival that it had dedicated the festival to a single theme. The festival showcased arts, crafts, and culture from the countries along the Silk Road.

Any musical endeavor by Yo-Yo Ma would not be complete without a recording. In 2002, Sony Classical released the first album featuring the Silk Road Ensemble. It is called *Silk Road Journeys: When Strangers Meet.* It contains traditional Mongolian,

Ma has explored links between musical traditions and instruments around the world. Here, he holds a Persian spiked fiddle.

Persian, and Chinese music, as well as compositions by numerous Silk Road Project participants.

The Silk Road recording was not Ma's only work in the recording studio in 2002. He was featured on the soundtrack to an artistic film called *Naqoyqatsi: Life as War*. The soundtrack is by composer Philip Glass. The score is written for solo cello, accompanied by orchestra. The film is a collection of images about the evils of technology, set to music. The music in the film never stops.

That year, Ma also released *Yo-Yo Ma Plays the Music of John Williams*. On the CD, Ma plays Williams's works for cello. Three of the pieces on the recording were written specifically for Yo-Yo Ma: a cello concerto, "Heartwood for Cello and Orchestra," and "Three Pieces for Solo Cello." Williams wrote the fourth piece, "Elegy for Cello and Orchestra," for the memorial service of the children of a friend.

During Ma's fourth year of directing the Silk Road Project, he agreed to stay on for another four years. Dr. Levin chose to step down from his post of curatorial director and offer his assistance as curatorial consultant. The Silk Road Project soon announced its 2002–2003 tour schedule, which included cities in Italy, Chicago, Las Vegas, cities in California, Vancouver, and Toronto.

By this point, the Silk Road Project was influencing Ma's solo career as well. Many of his appearances with major symphony orchestras featured music inspired by the Silk Road Project. In February 2003, Ma premiered a piece by Tan Dun called "The Map." It was written for cello and orchestra, accompanied by visual multimedia.

The piece was a hit with the audience at its premiere with the Boston Symphony Orchestra. "Tan Dun's 'The Map' is entertaining, instructive, valuable, and a crowd-pleaser," wrote a *Boston Globe* reviewer. "The audience at the world premiere last night, many from the younger visually-oriented generations, rewarded composer, soloist Yo-Yo Ma and the Boston Symphony Orchestra with a five-minute standing ovation."[15]

In late April and early May 2003, the Silk Road Ensemble finally traveled to Central Asia to give master classes and performances in the countries of Kazakhstan, the Kyrgyzstan, and Tajikistan.

Remarkably, even while trying to juggle his performing career with his duties as artistic director of the Silk Road Project, Ma still found time to explore different kinds of music. In April 2003, he released a recording that explored his cultural roots: not Chinese, but French.

"French music was in my earliest memories," Ma explained. "It's so in my blood. . . . It's what soul food is for some people."[16]

The CD, called *Paris: La Belle Époque*, features four works by French composers written around the turn of the twentieth century. None of the pieces were originally written for cello. Instead, they are pieces for violin and piano. One, the sonata by César Franck, has been played by cellists for decades. Ma arranged the other three pieces himself for cello and piano. He made the recording with friend and longtime recital partner Kathryn Stott. The two toured together during winter and spring 2003, performing pieces from the recording as well as other selections by composers from France, Russia, and Argentina.

Ma soon followed up his musical trip to France with an album dedicated to the music of Brazil, called *Obrigado Brazil.* The CD hit stores in July 2003. In February 2004, it was awarded a Grammy for Best Classical Crossover Album.

Ma's interest in Brazilian music had begun years earlier, when he heard it on the radio as a teen. This early interest was piqued when Ma was in South America working on his Piazzolla project. Ma kept in touch with a guitarist from the project, Oscar Castro-Neves. The two wanted to work together again, so Ma began listening to as much Brazilian music as he could. The ensemble swelled to include internationally acclaimed guitarists Sérgio and Odair Assad as well as vocalist Rosa Passos, pianist Kathryn Stott, and several other musicians. The group toured in support of the album in summer and fall 2003, including a stop in Tanglewood in July.

Tanglewood remains one of Ma's favorite places. His annual performances there date back to his son's infancy. "My son, Nicholas, was just three months old when I played at Tanglewood the first time," Ma said in June 2003, not long after Nicholas returned home from his second year at Harvard University.[17] The Mas now own a summer home near Tanglewood so that Yo-Yo can spend as much time as possible with his family during the summer months. During the year, Ma tours only during the week, reserving weekends for his family.

"The central core of my existence is my family,"

says Ma. "They feed me and give me so much. . . . Their love also allows me to really care about people and then be able to communicate feelings, ideas and ideals. They allow me . . . to touch an audience or have them understand what I am trying to convey and bring out the best in people."[18]

For Ma, music is about communication. He believes music can bring people together, and that exploring music of other cultures is a way to overcome national boundaries.[19] What kind of music will Yo-Yo Ma be playing in a few years? He may not even know himself. One thing is certain: Ma is likely to remain not only the world's foremost cellist but also its most enthusiastic musical explorer. "Being artistic," says Ma, "is going to the edge and then reporting back."[20]

Chronology

1955—Yo-Yo Ma born in Paris, France, on October 7.

1959—Begins studying cello with his father.

1962—Ma family moves to New York City.

1964—Enters the Pre-College Division of the Juilliard School; begins studying with faculty member Leonard Rose.

1968—Receives excellent reviews for performance of Saint-Saëns cello concerto with the San Francisco Little Symphony.

1971—Gives recital in New York's Carnegie Hall on May 6; graduates from Professional Children's School in June at age fifteen.

1972—Enters Harvard University.

1976—Graduates from Harvard with a bachelor of arts in humanities.

1978—Marries Jill Hornor; wins Avery Fisher Prize.

1980—Undergoes successful operation to correct curvature of the spine.

1983—Purchases cello made in 1733 by Italian maker Domenico Montagnana; first child, Nicholas, is born.

1984—Wins first Grammy Award, for recording of Bach cello suites; acquires Davidoff Stradivarius cello; principal cello teacher, Leonard Rose, dies.

1985—Daughter, Emily, is born; wins two Grammy Awards.

1986—Recording of Beethoven Cello Sonata No. 4 with Emanuel Ax wins Grammy for Best Chamber Music Performance.

1991—Plays concert of all six Bach suites in New York; receives honorary doctorate from Harvard University; plays "Begin Again Again" by Tod Machover on hypercello; father dies on August 28.

1992—Records best-selling album *Hush* with vocalist Bobby McFerrin.

1993—Visits Bushmen in Kalahari Desert in Africa; films documentary of trip called *Distant Echoes*.

1996—Releases best-selling album *Appalachia Waltz* with Edgar Meyer and Mark O'Connor.

1997—Featured on soundtrack of movie *Seven Years in Tibet*.

1998—*Soul of the Tango* wins Grammy for Best Classical Crossover Album; *Inspired by Bach* films shown on PBS; founds Silk Road Project.

1999—Releases *Solo*, album of solo cello music drawn from Silk Road Project; grabs headlines after leaving Montagnana cello in New York taxicab.

2000—Plays on Grammy-winning soundtrack for *Crouching Tiger, Hidden Dragon*; *Appalachian Journey* gains Ma his fourteenth Grammy Award.

2001—Silk Road Project begins Partner City Festival tour.

2002—Releases *Silk Road Journeys: When Strangers Meet*, first album featuring Silk Road Ensemble, and *Yo-Yo Ma Plays the Music of John Williams*.

2003—Releases two recordings, *Paris: La Belle Époque* and *Obrigado Brazil*.

Selected Discography

*Won Grammy Award   ****Won two Grammys**

*Obrigado Brazil, 2003

Paris: La Belle Époque, 2003

Silk Road Journeys: When Strangers Meet, 2002

Yo-Yo Ma Plays the Music of John Williams, 2002

Crouching Tiger, Hidden Dragon, 2000

Simply Baroque II, 2000

*Appalachian Journey, 2000

Dvořák: Piano Quartet No. 2, Sonatina in G, Romantic Pieces, 2000

Solo, 1999

Brahms: Piano Concerto No. 2, Cello Sonata Op. 78, 1999

Simply Baroque, 1999

Tavener: The Protecting Veil, 1998

Inspired by Bach: The Cello Suites, 1998

*Soul of the Tango, 1997

The Tango Lesson, 1997

Seven Years in Tibet, 1997

Tan Dun: Symphony 1997, 1997

**Premieres: Cello Concertos by Danielpour, Kirchner and Rouse, 1996

Appalachia Waltz, 1996

Schubert: Trout Quintet; Arpeggione Sonata, 1996

*Brahms, Beethoven, Mozart: Clarinet Trios, 1995

The New York Album, 1994

Beethoven, Schumann: Piano Quartets, 1994

Fauré: Piano Quartets, 1993

Made in America, 1993

Hush, 1992

*Prokofiev: Sinfonia Concertante; Tchaikovsky: Rococco Variations; Andante Cantabile, 1992

*Brahms: Cello Sonatas, 1992

*Brahms: The Piano Quartets, 1990

Shostakovich: Quartet No. 15; Gubaidulina: Rejoice, 1989

Anything Goes, 1989

*Barber: Cello Concerto; Britten: Symphony for Cello & Orchestra, 1989

Mozart: Adagio and Fugue in C Minor; Schubert: String Quartet No. 15, 1987

*Beethoven: Cello Sonata No. 4; Variations, 1986

*Elgar, Walton: Cello Concertos, 1985

Schubert: Quintet in C Major, 1985

*Brahms: Cello Sonatas in E minor and F, 1985

Beethoven: Cello Sonatas Nos. 3 & 5, 1984

Bolling: Suite for Cello and Jazz Piano Trio, 1984

Shostakovich, Kabalevsky: Cello Concertos, 1984

*Bach: Unaccompanied Cello Suites, 1983

Beethoven: Cello Sonatas, Op. 5, Nos. 1 & 2, 1983

Saint-Saëns, Lalo: Cello Concertos, 1983

Kreisler, Paganini: Works, 1983

Note: *Some listings represent Sony Classical reissues of previous Ma recordings.*

Chapter Notes

Chapter 1. Inspired by Bach

1. Richard Dyer, "Crossing Over: Yo-Yo Ma Makes Collaborative Music Films Out of Bach's Solo Cello Suites," *Boston Globe*, March 29, 1998, p. N1.

2. Bonnie Churchill, "'Inspired' Idea: Cellist Yo-Yo Ma Hopes to Widen the Audience for Classical Music with a Unique PBS Collaboration," *Boston Herald*, March 29, 1998, p. O41.

3. David Patrick Stearns, "The Sights Are No Match for the Sounds," *USA Today*, March 31, 1998, p. 3D.

4. Edith Eisler, "Continuity in Diversity," *Strings*, May/June 2001, p. 51.

Chapter 2. Choosing a "Big Instrument"

1. Marina Ma and John A. Rallo, *My Son, Yo-Yo* (Hong Kong: The Chinese University Press, 1995), p. 48.

2. Janet Tassel, "Yo-Yo Ma's Journeys," *Harvard Magazine*, March–April 2000. <http://www.harvard-magazine.com/issues/ma00/yoyoma.html> (March 2, 2003).

3. Ma and Rallo, p. 29.

4. David Blum, "Ma Energetico," *Strad*, January 1988, p. 21.

5. Ma and Rallo, p. 31.

6. David Blum, "A Process Larger Than Oneself," *New Yorker*, May 1, 1989, pp. 41–74. Reprinted in Blum, David. *Quintet: Five Journeys Toward Musical Fulfillment* (Ithaca N.Y.: Cornell University Press, 1998), p. 8.

7. Gale Research, *Contemporary Musicians*, Volume 2 (Farmington Hills, Mich.: The Gale Group, 1989). Reproduced in *Biography Resource Center*, 2002. <http://galenet.galegroup.com/servlet/BioRC> (May 8, 2002).

8. Ma and Rallo, p. 63.

9. Blum, *Strad*, p. 21.

10. Blum, *Quintet: Five Journeys Toward Musical Fulfillment*, p. 10.

11. Robert Sherman, "Celebrities Help École Française," *New York Times*, December 18, 1964.

12. Blum, *Quintet: Five Journeys Toward Musical Fulfillment*, p. 10.

13. Ibid., p. 10.

14. Ma and Rallo, pp. 101–104.

15. Blum, *Quintet: Five Journeys Toward Musical Fulfillment*, p. 10.

16. Richard Thorne, "The Magic of Yo-Yo Ma," *Saturday Review*, July 1981, p. 56.

17. Ma and Rallo, pp. 97–98.

Chapter 3. From High School to Harvard

1. Lloyd Schwartz, "On Tour with Yo-Yo Ma," *Harvard Magazine*, January–February 1982, p. 38.

2. Susan Elliott, "Ax & Ma: Duo Extraordinary," *Musical America*, May 1990, p. 23.

3. David Blum, "Ma Energetico," *Strad*, January 1988, p. 22.

4. Ed Siegel, "Playing the Full Human Range," *Boston Globe*, August 6, 1995, p. B29.

5. Richard Thorne, "The Magic of Yo-Yo Ma," *Saturday Review*, July 1981, p. 56.

6. Janet Tassel, "Yo-Yo Ma's Journeys," *Harvard Magazine*, March–April 2000. <http://www.harvard-magazine.com/issues/ma00/yoyoma.html> (March 2, 2003).

7. Schwartz, p. 38.

8. Marina Ma and John A. Rallo, *My Son, Yo-Yo* (Hong Kong: The Chinese University Press, 1995), pp. 124–128.

9. Edith Eisler, "Yo-Yo Ma: Music from the Soul," *Strings*, May/June 1992, p. 50.

10. Anne Inglis, "In Pursuit of Excellence," *Strad*, May 1984, p. 30.

11. Tassel, *Harvard Magazine*.

12. Herbert Kupferberg, "Yo-Yo Ma," *Stereo Review*, April 1990, p. 71.

13. "Yo-Yo's Way with the Strings," *Time*, January 19, 1981, p. 55.

14. Tassel, *Harvard Magazine*.

15. David Blum, "A Process Larger Than Oneself," *New Yorker*, May 1, 1989, pp. 41–74. Reprinted in Blum, David. *Quintet: Five Journeys Toward Musical Fulfillment* (Ithaca: N.Y. Cornell University Press, 1998), p. 14.

16. Inglis, p. 31.

17. Blum, *Quintet: Five Journeys Toward Musical Fulfillment*, p. 14.

18. Tassel, *Harvard Magazine*.

19. Schwartz, p. 38.

20. Blum, *Quintet: Five Journeys Toward Musical Fulfillment*, p. 15.

21. Schwartz, p. 39.

22. Ibid., p. 38.

Chapter 4. An Emerging Star

1. Lloyd Schwartz, "On Tour with Yo-Yo Ma," *Harvard Magazine*, January–February 1982, p. 40.

2. David Blum, "A Process Larger Than Oneself," *New Yorker*, May 1, 1989, pp. 41–74. Reprinted in Blum, David. *Quintet: Five Journeys Toward Musical Fulfillment* (Ithaca N.Y.: Cornell University Press, 1998), p. 20.

3. Schwartz, p. 37.

4. Blum, *Quintet: Five Journeys Toward Musical Fulfillment*, p. 18.

5. Ibid., p. 19.

6. Joseph Horowitz, "Yo-Yo Ma Plays Cello," *New York Times*, April 17, 1978, p. C19.

7. Blum, *Quintet: Five Journeys Toward Musical Fulfillment*, p. 20.

8. Herbert Kupferberg, "Yo-Yo Ma," *Stereo Review*, April 1990, p. 72.

9. Bruce Handy and Daniel S. Levy, "Yo-Yo Ma's Suite Life?" *Time*, March 23, 1998, pp. 83ff.

10. Janet Tassel, "Yo-Yo Ma's Journeys," *Harvard Magazine*, March–April 2000. <http://www.harvard-magazine.com/issues/ma00/yoyoma.html> (March 2, 2003).

11. Heidi Waleson, "Two Soloists Make a Different Kind of Duo," *New York Times*, November 20, 1988, p. 27.

12. Richard Thorne, "The Magic of Yo-Yo Ma," *Saturday Review*, July 1981, p. 58.

13. Blum, *Quintet: Five Journeys Toward Musical Fulfillment*, p. 21.

14. Schwartz, p. 35.

15. "Yo-Yo's Way with the Strings," *Time*, January 19, 1981, p. 55.

16. Schwartz, p. 38.

17. Thorne, p. 58.

18. Schwartz, p. 35.

19. Anne Inglis, "In Pursuit of Excellence," *Strad*, May 1984, p. 32.

20. Blum, *Quintet: Five Journeys Toward Musical Fulfillment*, p. 20.

21. Schwartz, p. 40.

22. Tim Page, "Leonard Rose Benefit," *New York Times*, November 1, 1986, p. 11.

Chapter 5. Yo-Yo Ma Branches Out

1. David Blum, "A Process Larger Than Oneself," *New Yorker*, May 1, 1989, pp. 41–74. Reprinted in Blum, David. *Quintet: Five Journeys Toward Musical Fulfillment* (Ithaca N.Y.: Cornell University Press, 1998), p. 20.

2. Edith Eisler, "Yo-Yo Ma: Music from the Soul," *Strings*, May/June 1992, p. 50.

3. Ed Siegel, "Playing the Full Human Range," *Boston Globe*, August 6, 1995, p. B29.

4. Bernard Holland, "Ma and Ax Perform Bolcom," *New York Times*, May 8, 1990, p. 19.

5. Susan Elliott, "Ax & Ma: Duo Extraordinary," *Musical America*, May 1990, p. 24.

6. Richard Dyer, "Ma and McFerrin: A Match Made in Tanglewood," *Boston Globe*, January 19, 1991, p. 18p.

7. Eisler, p. 51.

8. Blum, *Quintet: Five Journeys Toward Musical Fulfillment*, p. 33.

9. Eisler, pp. 52–53.

10. Ibid., p. 53.

11. Ibid., p. 54.

12. Ibid.

13. Philip Kennicott, "A Born Idealist," *Gramophone*, April 1996, p. 17.

14. Richard Dyer, "Crossing Over: Yo-Yo Ma Makes Collaborative Music Films Out of Bach's Solo Cello Suites," *Boston Globe*, March 29, 1998, p. N1.

15. Bonnie Churchill, "'Inspired' Idea; Cellist Yo-Yo Ma Hopes to Widen the Audience for Classical Music with a Unique PBS Collaboration," *Boston Herald*, March 29, 1998, p. O41.

16. Mitch Potter, "Inspired by Bach," *Toronto Star*, October 18, 1997, p. J1.

17. Eisler, p. 52.

Chapter 6. Seeking New Musical Forms

1. Philip Kennicott, "A Born Idealist," *Gramophone*, April 1996, p. 16.

2. Justin Davidson, "Have Cello, Will Travel," *Newsday*, November 30, 1997, p. D10.

3. Janet Tassel, "Yo-Yo Ma's Journeys," *Harvard Magazine*, March–April 2000. <http://www.harvard-magazine. com/issues/ma00/yoyoma.html> (March 2, 2003).

4. Kennicott, p. 16.

5. Beverly Schuch, "Internationally Known Cellist Yo-Yo Ma Continues to Expand His Musical Horizons," *CNN Pinnacle*, August 4, 2001 (transcript).

6. Matthew Gurewitsch and Philip Herrera, "Master Ma," *Town & Country*, February 1998, pp. 47ff.

7. Peter Goddard, "Yo-Yo Ma," *Toronto Star*, January 6, 1996, p. K1.

8. Tan Shzr Ee, "Snake? It's OK, Take Me to the Desert," *Straits Times* (Singapore), March 12, 1999, pp. 1, L3.

9. Phan Ming Yen, "Yo-Yo Ma's Whirlwind Schedule," *Straits Times* (Singapore), November 18, 1993, pp. 1, L2, L4.

10. Ibid.

11. David Balakrishnan, "String Players' Waltz," *Strings*, March/April 1997, p. 34.

12. Jamie James, "Yo-Yo Ma May Be a National Institution, But He Continues to Reinvent Himself," *New York Times*, December 31, 1995.

13. Heidi Waleson, "Classical Meets Bluegrass on New Sony Album," *Billboard*, August 10, 1996, p. 1ff.

Chapter 7. An Expanding Worldview

1. Matthew Gurewitsch and Philip Herrera, "Master Ma," *Town & Country*, February 1998, pp. 47ff.

2. Daniel Webster, "Three Cello Concertos of the Decade," *Philadelphia Inquirer*, January 6, 1996, p. D8.

3. Peter Goddard, "Yo-Yo Ma," *Toronto Star*, January 6, 1996, p. K1.

4. Jamie James, "Yo-Yo Ma May Be a National Institution, But He Continues to Reinvent Himself," *New York Times*, December 31, 1995.

5. Justin Davidson, "Have Cello, Will Travel," *Newsday*, November 30, 1997, p. D10.

6. James R. Oestreich, "Bach's Life in Six Suites as Presented by Yo-Yo Ma," *New York Times*, March 16, 1998.

7. Richard Dyer, "As TV, Bach Films' Reach Exceeds Their Grasp," *Boston Globe*, March 29, 1998, p. N4.

8. Janet Tassel, "Yo-Yo Ma's Journeys," *Harvard Magazine*, March–April 2000. <http://www.harvard-magazine.com/issues/ma00/yoyoma.html> (March 2, 2003).

9. Terry Teachout, "At the Top of His Powers," *Time*, March 23, 1998, p. 83ff (inset).

10. David Patrick Stearns, "The Sights Are No Match for the Sounds," *USA Today*, March 31, 1998, p. 3D.

11. "People in the News," *U.S. News & World Report*, April 13, 1998, p. 16.

Chapter 8. Traveling the Silk Road

1. Silk Road Project, <http://www.silkroadproject.org> (February 15, 2003).

2. James R. Oestreich, "Making a 1712 Cello Sound Less Modern," *New York Times*, February 20, 1999, p. B7.

3. Ibid.

4. Ibid.

5. Helen Wallace, "Out of Place in Baroque World," London *Times*, April 27, 1999.

6. Edith Eisler, "Continuity in Diversity," *Strings*, May/June 2001, p. 50.

7. Janet Tassel, "Yo-Yo Ma's Journeys," *Harvard Magazine*, March–April 2000. <http://www.harvard-magazine.com/issues/ma00/yoyoma.html> (March 2, 2003).

8. Tim Page, "Yo-Yo Ma: Simply the Best," *Washington Post*, January 25, 1999, C1.

9. Tim Ashley, "A Cello and a Nice Chat," London *Guardian*, November 3, 1999.

10. Beverly Schuch, "Internationally Known Cellist Yo-Yo Ma Continues to Expand His Musical Horizons," *CNN Pinnacle*, August 4, 2001 (transcript).

11. Beth Gardiner, Associated Press, October 16, 1999.

Chapter 9. When Strangers Meet

1. Lesley Valdes, "Traveling the Silk Route," *American Record Guide*, November/December 2001, pp. 44ff.

2. Ken Smith, "When Strangers Meet," *Strad*, February 2002. <http://www.classicalmusicworld.com/home.asp?magazine=archives> (March 3, 2003).

3. Gloria Goodale, "Finding a Musical Route Between East and West," *Christian Science Monitor*, March 9, 2001, p. 18.

4. John Pitcher, "For He's a Jolly Good Cello," *Washington Post*, June 2, 2000, C1.

5. Smith, *Strad.*

6. Bradley Bambarger, "Classical: Keeping Score," *Billboard*, March 3, 2001.

7. Melinda Bargreen, "Cellist Yo-Yo Ma's Silk Road Project Paves Way for Cross-Cultural Exchanges," *Seattle Times*, May 5, 2002, p. K1.

8. Michael Church, "Wealth of Nations," London *Independent*, May 10, 2002, pp. 22–23.

9. Valdes, pp. 44ff.

10. Church, pp. 22–23.

11. Martin Steinberg, "Musical Shepherd Yo-Yo Ma Takes His Silk Road Caravan into New York's Carnegie Hall," Associated Press, May 9, 2002.

12. Susan Osmond, "Yo-Yo Ma's Silk Road Project," *World & I*, April 2002, pp. 70ff.

13. Philip Kennicott, "It's Not So Smooth on Ma's Silk Road," *Washington Post*, October 22, 2001, p. C5.

14. Melinda Bargreen, "Yo-Yo Ma & Co. Strike Gold," *American Record Guide*, September/October 2002, pp. 6ff.

15. Richard Dyer, "A Composer Shows His Roots," *Boston Globe*, February 21, 2003.

16. T.J. Medrek, "Classical Music: Ma's 'Map' Includes a Return to France," *Boston Herald*, January 17, 2003, p. S09.

17. Richard Dyer, "Classical Music: With Ear for Diversity, Cellist Yo-Yo Ma Has the World on a String," *Boston Globe*, June 22, 2003, p. N6.

18. Richard Turp, "Ma's Magical Music Tour: Cellist and Collaborators Combine Imaginations for Film Series on Bach Suites," *Calgary Herald*, June 21, 1997, p. I8.

19. Yo-Yo Ma, "Vision Statement," Silk Road Project. <http://www.silkroadproject.org> (September 12, 2003).

20. Justin Davidson, "Have Cello, Will Travel," *Newsday*, November 30, 1997, p. D10.

Further Reading

Books

Blum, David. "A Process Larger Than Oneself." In *Quintet: Five Journeys Toward Musical Fulfillment.* Ithaca, N.Y.: Cornell University Press, 1998. First published in *New Yorker*, May 1, 1989.

Ma, Marina, and John A. Rallo. *My Son, Yo-Yo.* Hong Kong: The Chinese University Press, 1995.

Magazines and Newspapers

Eisler, Edith. "Yo-Yo Ma: Music from the Soul." *Strings*, May/June 1992, pp. 48–54.

———. "Continuity in Diversity." *Strings*, May/June 2001, pp. 47–54.

Gurewitsch, Matthew and Philip Herrera. "Master Ma." *Town & Country*, February 1998, p. 47ff.

Handy, Bruce and Daniel S. Levy. "Yo-Yo Ma's Suite Life?" *Time*, March 23, 1998, p. 83ff.

Oestreich, James R. "At Lunch with Yo-Yo Ma." *New York Times*, September 21, 1994, p. C1.

Osmond, Susan. "Yo-Yo Ma's Silk Road Project." *World & I*, April 2002, pp. 70ff.

Sand, Barbara L. "Extending the Boundaries." *Strad*, November 1996, pp. 1120–1125.

Tassel, Janet. "Yo-Yo Ma's Journeys," *Harvard Magazine*, March-April 2000. Available at <http://www.harvard-magazine.com/issues/ma00/yoyoma.html>.

Video

Yo-Yo Ma: Inspired by Bach, Vol. 3. "Struggle for Hope," dir. Niv Fichman; "Six Gestures," dir. Patricia Rozema. Produced by Rhombus Media. Sony Classical, 1998, VHS/DVD.

Internet Addresses

The Silk Road Project
<http://www.silkroadproject.org>

Yo-Yo Ma Official Site
<http://www.yo-yoma.com/>

Yo-Yo Ma: Inspired by Bach
<http://www.sonyclassical.com/music/63203/index2.html>

Index

Page numbers for photographs are in **boldface** type.